AF446440

Notes / Ex

"A powerful and compelling account of the extraordinary dedication and resilience of election officials who make our democracy happen. Wu illustrates firsthand how these unsung heroes in our election offices ensure voting is as convenient as possible, especially in response to challenges posed by the global pandemic. An essential read for anyone seeking to understand the work behind 'making elections work.'"

—Keara Mendez, Director of Advocacy, Center for Tech and Civic Life

"This valuable book provides a rare look at the inner workings of an election process. The circumstances make it especially intriguing, for it's the 2020 fall election in Orange County, California, beset by wildfires, voter intimidation, attempted sabotage, and shooter and bomb threats. Author Jackie Wu was on the front lines, and she chronicles this historic election in passionate detail."

—David Aretha, editor, *Civil Rights Chronicle*

"Jackie Wu offers a fascinating insider's perspective on the essential work election workers do in running U.S. elections as well as the obstacles and dangers they encounter. With over 30 years of experience working for state legislators, candidates, and nonprofits, I have witnessed firsthand their dedication and resilience. This book offers a glimpse into the lives of the hardworking public employees who make democracy possible for us all."

—Bill Wong, Democratic Strategist and Amazon best-selling
author of *Better to Win: Hardball Lessons in Leadership,
Influence* and the *Craft of Politics*

"Having dedicated years working to make voting easier for everyone, I am thrilled to endorse a book telling the story of election officials in Orange County during the 2020 Presidential Election. Their innovative efforts to improving the voter experience positively impacted the democratic process, resulting in historic voter turnout – even amidst a pandemic. An eye-opening read and a success story of providing accessible voting for all."

—Whitney Quesenbery, Executive Director, Center for Civic Design

"A rare first-hand account by a dedicated public servant who has worked tirelessly to keep our democracy working. Describing a time when public agencies faced unprecedented challenges, this book details how expert, nonpartisan, hardworking election officials like Ms. Wu were responsive to voters' needs and ensured that every voter had access to the ballot box."

—Sam Oliker-Friedland, Executive Director,
Institute for Responsive Government

"As a fellow Asian American election official, I have personally experienced the unique obstacles and triumphs that come with this profession. This book will serve as a source of inspiration and empowerment for current and future generations of election workers. I highly recommend *On the Front Lines of Democracy* to anyone seeking a deeper understanding of the craft, dedication and sacrifice of election officials."

—Tommy Gong, Deputy County Clerk-Recorder, Contra Costa County

"With perspectives both professional and personal, Jackie Wu shares a vital and timely exploration of the immense hurdles and threats faced by courageous, dedicated election officials in the 2020 election, providing invaluable insights into what happens behind the scenes in safeguarding the electoral process."

—Brian Green, political consultant and author
of *Rail Tales: Adventures on Public Transit*

"*On the Front Lines of Democracy* presents a month-by-month survey of events in 2020 America that melds insights into Jackie Wu's life with observations of voting rights. While its focus is on what it's like to be an election official overseeing this right to vote, Wu even more importantly documents the daily struggles for preserving rights that have been eroded in other countries. Very highly recom-mended for libraries, for readers interested in insights about democracy, and for book clubs."

—D. Donovan, Senior Reviewer, *Midwest Book Review*

ON THE FRONT LINES OF
DEMOCRACY

ON THE FRONT LINES OF

DEMOCRACY

An Election Official's Story of Protecting the Vote in 2020

JACKIE WU

Published by Golden Torch Press

To contact the author about speaking, consulting, or ordering books in bulk, visit www.jwuconsulting.com.

ISBN (paperback): 979-8-9911228-0-1

ISBN (ebook): 979-8-9911228-1-8

Editor: David Aretha

Book design: Christy Day, Constellation Book Services

Library of Congress Control Number: 2024915779

Printed in the United States of America

To past, present, and future election officials. Thank you for your tireless efforts in preserving the fundamental right to vote and ensuring elections are transparent, accessible, and conducted with integrity. As unsung heroes who work behind the scenes to make sure ballots are sent out on time and counted accurately, we cannot thank you enough for making sure our voices are heard and that our democracy continues to flourish.

To the family members, loved ones, and friends of election officials whose support makes it possible for us to dedicate our lives to ensuring democracy lives on. We are forever indebted to you for your patience, resilience, and love as we put our lives on pause to ensure elections are administered well and that every eligible voter can cast a ballot.

CONTENTS

PREFACE   1

MARCH 2020   9
Primary Election Day   11
The Shutdowns and Changes Begin   16

APRIL 2020   19
In Search of Guidance on How to Run Elections in a Pandemic   21
My Role in the Office and Life Outside of the Office   24
2020 Westminster Recall Special Election   27

MAY 2020   31
Learning to Manage a Recount in a Pandemic   33
Executive Order N-64-20   35
Preparations for the 2020 General Election Begin   37

JUNE 2020   41
Creating the COVID-19 Election Response Report   43
Election Officials: Essential but Not Invincible   47

JULY 2020   49
Developing Election Worker Training Under COVID-19   51
The Registrar Returns   56
Candidate Filing and Translations Begin   58

AUGUST 2020   63
Launching Online Training Under COVID-19   65
If Health Is Wealth, Then I Was Poor in 2020   69
Modified Election Administration Waiver   73

Notifying the Public About Voting Under COVID-19   75

Planning Pop-up Mobile Voting   76

"How is Orange County planning to run the 2020 General?"   79

SEPTEMBER 2020   **81**

Sporting Venues Step Up for Democracy   83

A Right to Public Observation   86

Increasing Misinformation and Conspiracy Theories   88

What Would You Sacrifice for Democracy?   95

The Race to Train 1,500 Election Workers   97

MAGA Target #1: Election Officials   103

Language Access for Every Language at Every Voting Location   106

OCTOBER 2020   **109**

Partnerships Between the Election Office and Media   111

Fake Ballot Boxes Are Not Fake News (Unfortunately)   116

Active Shooter Worries and Wildfire Risks   119

A Fake Vote Center Is Not Fake News (Unfortunately)   125

Command Center Operations   128

Pop-up Voting Begins   133

NOVEMBER 2020   **137**

The Day Before Election Day   139

E-0: Election Day   142

A Quiet Reflection and Acceptance   143

Election Morning Begins   146

7 a.m.: The Polls Are Now Open   152

You're in or Urine?   153

Westminster Bomb Scare   155

Election Fashion: American Flags and Campaign Attire   158

Leave Your Guns at Home; Don't Take Them to the Vote Center   161

"Meet at the Election Office for the Rally"   163

Signs of Hope and Positivity   165

8 p.m: The Polls Are Now Closed   167

Collection Centers   170

Internal Sorting   172

Election Night Guests   173

Closing the Doors on Election Night   175

Afterword   179

Resources and How to Get Involved   182

Acknowledgments   187

Photos   189

PREFACE

My American story begins with my parents. More specifically, my story begins with my parents' escape from the Vietnam War and the destruction left in Southeast Asia long after the war officially ended. The highly unpopular Vietnam War wasted valuable resources and, most tragically, destroyed countless lives. After escaping Vietnam during the turmoil, my parents met in a refugee camp in Indonesia, where their respective rickety boats safely docked after making the treacherous journey.

Both recount their experiences as if this journey was no special deal and prefer not to talk about it. It takes an enormous amount of courage and bravery to leave everything you know behind and risk your life in the hopes of a better life and a better future. In their words, it was just something people at the time did and it was not anything special. That's how I largely view my voting rights and civic engagement work. Then, I realized there weren't many stories of election officials being told and I knew I had to be part of the change I wanted to see.

When I was first told stories about what life was like for my parents in that camp, I was shocked to learn details like how my calm and happy-go-lucky dad carried a machete to cut overgrown branches to get around the refugee camp. At some point, his path crossed with my mom's. They were teenagers in love against the backdrop of a makeshift city for refugees who fled bullets and bombs in the jungle. Love and hope in a place where both were in short supply. No matter how bleak things seemed, they persisted.

Fortunately, both were eventually accepted by the United States as refugees in the early 1980s, but they would be going to different coasts. My mother went to California to be received by extended family, and my dad was sponsored by a church in Connecticut. Unfazed by the distance and figuring out how to travel across a new country in which he was not fluent in the dominant language, my dad ultimately followed her to California without the assistance of modern technology. After all, they had just escaped a war. What else could the world possibly throw at them?

I can't say that I would have been able to maintain the resolve and hope that my parents exhibited during all the years that their futures remained in limbo, with little comfort and security to bolster their faith. My extended family immigrated to the United States as refugees with nothing to their name. They left all they knew and longed for the promise of opportunity in a new land that they could start anew in.

That leap of faith would be dizzying for many Americans to experience, including me. When they were just children themselves, my parents resolved that they would strive against all odds to provide better opportunities for themselves and their future children. *Somewhere is better than here and we're willing to risk death to find it,* they must have thought. I was the first in my family to be born in the United States, and I have always been conflicted about the circumstances of how my American story began.

I recognize that my very existence was possible through a sequence of events that stemmed from very turbulent political circumstances that entailed countless infringements of basic human rights and a severe lack of civil rights. Beyond that disturbing concept, the country that I was raised in, have worked for, and place in such high regard as a nation where public servants toil tirelessly to protect democracy was the very aggressor of the conflict in Vietnam. However, if Vietnam had not been in a civil war, would my parents have fled the country and met in a refugee camp? Would they have been reunited in the United States if its refugee resettlement policies were different? I don't think so, and I wouldn't have been blessed with the life I have lived so far.

This specific narrative is an aspect of my identity that informs my opinion of why it is imperative to vigilantly protect the right of the people to express their values and opinions through voting. Anything that suppresses the vote is in essence suppressing the will of the people. If suppression is the method by which power is obtained, then that power is illegitimate. The people have all of the power and always will.

On April 30, 1975, Saigon fell and so did democracy in Vietnam when a tank rammed through the locked iron gates of Saigon's Presidential Palace. Forty-one million lives in Vietnam and the course of world history would change forever. When election denialists forced their way into the U.S. Capitol with the intent to overthrow the government, I feared that we were witnessing the demise of our democracy and history was being repeated. Fortunately, these insurrectionists failed in their pursuit and democracy continues to live to this day in the U.S. Yet, we cannot take it for granted. We cannot take our election workers who are on the front lines of democracy every day, election year or not, for granted.

Each election worker has their own story, and each story is just as powerful. Choosing to be on the front lines of democracy is not an easy decision. The reasons that individuals stay dedicated to the mission of free and fair elections are personal. Their passion for helping others and protecting the principles of democracy must be stronger than any challenges that they might face.

Those who have never been in this position may not fully understand the weight of achieving the goal (in this case, of conducting a free and fair election) by *all means* and to the necessarily high standard set by our government. Former Orange County Registrar of Voters Neal Kelley is someone who fully understands this as he was relentless in his pursuit of advancing election administration to create the most accessible, positive, and efficient experience for voters.

Neal was the highly respected chief election official in Orange County, California from 2005 to 2022. During his time, election administration in Orange County was seen as the gold standard for administering elections throughout the United States. Despite the contentious politics that Orange County is known for, Neal had a strong reputation as a fair nonpartisan election administrator. Unafraid of innovation and technology, Orange County often served as a testing ground for best practices from the private sector, the academic field, and the community. Neal's impact and contributions to the election administration in Orange County and the United States will be felt for a long time.

I was fortunate to work under Neal's leadership at the Orange County Registrar of Voters as the Community Outreach Manager. I was responsible for overseeing translations, language access, community outreach, media, social media, legislation, training, and pop-up mobile voting. The most impactful experience I had during my time there was planning and administration of the 2020 Presidential General Election. This election's voter turnout was 87.3% in Orange County, which was the highest voter turnout since the 1950s. An incredible feat on its own, it was even more impressive considering the circumstances that the election was conducted under:

- ★ Wildfires that limited and prevented voting access

- ★ Fake voting locations and ballot drop boxes

- ★ Ballot drop boxes set on fire

- ★ "Stop the Steal" protests at election offices

- ★ Unprecedented active shooter threats

- ★ Bomb threats at voting locations

- ★ Gun enthusiasts who threatened to intimidate voters at voting locations

- ★ Heightened risk of violence and instability due to a multitude of concurrent, overlapping political demonstrations and increasing polarization

- ★ Heavy scrutiny by the public and media

- ★ Misinformation on social media in multiple languages

- ★ Long lines for in-person voting because of misinformation spread about vote-by-mail ballots

- ★ Delayed mailings due to the U.S. Postal Service being overwhelmed

- ★ Unrelenting pressure from political parties, candidates, and campaigns

- ★ Election observers from international watchdog organizations present to monitor and report any suspicious threats to corrupt democracy
- ★ The threat of contracting COVID-19 in its deadliest days
- ★ Encountering thousands of voters each day before there were COVID-19 vaccines
- ★ The fear of passing COVID-19 to family and loved ones because of my exposure
- ★ Changing nearly every aspect of in-person voting and ballot processing due to COVID-19

One need not look any further than election officials to find some of the most dedicated proponents of democracy. Though they aren't often in the spotlight (nor do they seek it out), they are deserving of respect and support. Election officials are on the front lines of democracy; without their commitment, society as we know it would be very different.

Election officials are found in every corner of the United States, working quietly and diligently to ensure we receive ballots and nonpartisan election materials on time and elections are conducted securely and with integrity.

I wrote this book to shed light on what it's like to be an election official. I share what I experienced during the 2020 election cycle from my perspective as a former election official from Orange County, California. There are many more stories to be told, and I hope more election officials will share theirs.

I hope that this book will inspire readers to consider a career in election administration or serve as an election worker. We all have a role to play in protecting our democracy and ensuring every voice is heard. Thank you for reading my story.

MARCH 2020

PRIMARY ELECTION DAY

Election workers are natural planners, familiar with preparing for unlimited possibilities, challenges, and outcomes. An ideal candidate is someone who not only has a plan A but also a plan B, plan C, and an absolute fallback option. Yet, anyone who has worked in an elections office can tell you that there's always a surprise on Election Day that no one was prepared for.

I remember being stunned by the question the reporter asked me on Election Day for the 2020 Primary Election. There was so much buildup as it was a highly controversial election with both Donald Trump and Joe Biden vying to be presidential candidates for their respective political parties. I had not anticipated being presented with a health-related inquiry.

It felt like time stopped, and both my heart stopped beating and I stopped breathing.

The reporter seemed rather unfazed by my flustered reaction. "What are you doing to protect poll workers and voters from COVID-19?" they repeated.

I paused for a moment, feeling slightly bewildered. Election Day for the March 3, 2020 Presidential Primary Election was the first time I was asked about COVID-19's impact on our election staff and voter safety. My reaction to the reporter's question was highly uncommon for me.

I was accustomed to not knowing what could be waiting for me whenever I answered the Media Line for the Orange County Registrar of Voters (OCROV). As the lead media staff liaison for the office, I had the responsibility of delivering satisfactory, competent answers to reporters in a timely manner and usually did so without much trouble. I've had considerable experience in crafting apt responses to unexpected questions, but a few inquiries have momentarily left me at a loss for words.

In my professional and personal life, I have a reputation for being able to remain calm even under stressful situations, which certainly came in handy in my role as a senior manager who often had to speak with media outlets like CNN, Reuters, Associated Press, Fox News, etc., and candidates whose races garnered national attention and involved millions of dollars in campaign money. If elected, these candidates would have a significant impact on California, the United States, and potentially the world.

At the time, COVID-19 was just a foreign "flu-like" virus that much of the American public understood to be primarily China's problem and had only recently made its way to the United States in the form of a few odd, seemingly isolated cases. Its pandemic status was not realized by many Americans and no official health guidance was provided yet.

Our office already had a lot on its plate—a much-anticipated and controversial presidential primary election, the roll-out of new voting equipment after the previous system was phased out after fifteen years of use, and the transition from the traditional neighborhood polling place model of voting to Vote Centers.

Voters could go to any Vote Center, with expanded days and hours of operation, instead of only one polling place on Election Day.

After consulting internally, I let the reporter know that our office could not comment on public health matters and referred them to the Orange County Health Care Agency. This reporter's question was only one of numerous calls that the OCROV office had been receiving from media, observers, and political parties, and I had to handle what I thought were more pressing matters at the time.

A pop-up voting mobile unit that I was responsible for was overwhelmed with over three thousand voters at the University of California, Irvine (UC Irvine) campus, a large local university with more than 35,000 students. Many of them were students who had not registered to vote before the registration deadline and needed to go through special processing in order to cast their ballot. I recall feeling helpless as I campaigned for more staff and resources to be sent to my pop-up voting team. None were available, and I remember feeling like I had failed my team as their leader.

I retreated back to my office, and my disbelief and disappointment in myself grew as my team sent updates, photos, and videos of the never-ending line. A key memory of Election Night was hearing from a team member that our signature inflatable "I Voted" sticker unceremoniously deflated when the electricity needs overwhelmed our small generators while there were long lines of eager voters and media reporters looking on. Fortunately, UC Irvine allowed us to use their larger generator for the rest of Election Day.

Many other Vote Centers faced the problem of too many voters waiting until the last minute to vote. We could do nothing at this point. Despite some Vote Centers being open for ten days leading up to Election Day and all voters receiving a vote-by-mail ballot a month prior, many voters waited until Election Day to cast their ballot. Naturally, this resulted in having to wait to vote, and, as much as we urged voters to vote early, some intentionally waited until the last minute to decide who to vote for in the presidential primary election.

Please vote early to avoid lines and frustration. Most election workers try to do everything they can to ensure you have a positive voter experience, but voting equipment resources and time is finite.

California law states that voting operations cannot end before the last voter who was in line by the close of the polls (8 p.m. on Election Night) has finished casting their ballot. For a major election, the last voting location would typically close around 10 p.m., and election workers could be working until 3 a.m. to sort returning ballots and organize returning equipment.

If you want to see what dedication to democracy looks like, I encourage you to observe this process on Election Night at your local elections office. Many of the workers you see have toiled for long hours in the office, away from their family and friends for months, to ensure free, fair, and secure elections. The many, many sleepless nights. The missed birthdays, missed kids' sports events, and missed firsts that they'll never get back.

The reason why election workers can devote so much of themselves to their work is because of their loved ones. Nothing matters more than making sure that everyone has a chance to vote and that the election is administered accurately, effectively, and efficiently. They are exhausted, but they do not give up. Elections are heavily scrutinized, and the public and media's attention is squarely focused on election results on Election Night, which never seems to come fast enough.

Neal had begun thinking about bringing Vote Centers to Orange County in the early 2010s, and he officially brought the initiative to the Orange County Board of Supervisors for a vote in 2017. The Board of Supervisors did not pass it the first time, but Neal is not the type who gives up easily. In 2019, he brought the policy back up for consideration, and it passed unanimously.

Ensuring the smooth implementation of Vote Centers was critical to disprove the naysayers who parroted unfounded fears. I'm proud to share that the March 3, 2020 Presidential Primary Election had the highest voter turnout in a presidential primary election since 2000. Vote Centers were officially a success, which would cement its future as the model of voting in Orange County for years to come.

THE SHUTDOWNS AND CHANGES BEGIN

As we reeled from the chaos and excitement of the primary election, the news began to fill with reports of how serious COVID-19 was and how quickly it was spreading. It wasn't clear to what extent COVID-19 would change election operations and our lives at the time. We were just trying to do our jobs and finish counting ballots.

County government officials finally issued guidance on COVID-19 on March 15, 2020, in the middle of election canvass operations. If you are not familiar with the election canvass process, this is when all ballots are processed, verified, and counted. Voters are given the opportunity to "cure" any signature issues for a fixed period of time after Election Day; for example, a voter has the option to remedy issues arising from an unsigned ballot or a signature mismatch. Election offices cannot certify election results until this period passes and the offices complete other necessary requirements, such as post-election audits, to ensure the accuracy of the results.

Governor Gavin Newsom issued a stay-at-home order on March 19, 2020, less than two weeks after the primary election. Things began to move quickly after that. All OCROV employee events were canceled, and we began to see temporary staff over the age of sixty-five leave their positions as the State recognized seniors as a vulnerable population. Historically, seniors have been a significant portion of election workers. While we were able to manage the post-election canvass with less staff, this lack of staffing would prove to be more difficult later on.

Knowledge about COVID-19 and how to deal with it changed daily. For our staff, it was hard enough to keep up with the public health news as private citizens, but we also had the enormous responsibility, as election officials, to certify election results with many candidates, campaign staff, political parties, media outlets, and voters anxiously waiting and wanting to get inside of our office.

We did our best to move things forward and ensure everyone's safety, despite the uncertainty and anxiety of being in a public health crisis that blindsided the entire world. People looked to us and other government workers as being in charge and knew what to do. In reality, we were figuring it out along the way and trying to keep a brave and professional face to not let others down.

Fortunately, Neal started sending out periodic emails to provide updates on COVID-19 from local, state, and federal authorities. These were incredibly helpful as they provided consistent updates, and all staff across the department received the same messaging, which reduced confusion and provided direction.

One of the first COVID-19 emails indicated swift actions to protect our office and staff. We closed our doors to the public, but the public could still make appointments to receive assistance and either call or email staff. Normally, our office took great pride in being accessible to the public, media, campaigns, etc. so this partial lockdown was very unusual. However, these were unusual times, and it felt like every day brought new challenges that we had never anticipated.

As for post-election observation, we quickly mobilized to set up a remote observation system. Thanks to our dedicated IT team, we were among the first (if not the first) elections office to offer this service to the public to provide transparency and access to the elections process while maintaining public health and safety guidelines.

The cleaning and disinfectant supplies returned from the Vote Centers were an unintentional blessing. As these items began to be sold out and unavailable in stores, we had a small supply in our warehouse. However, the surplus evidently would not be enough for future elections, and our Administrative team began planning ahead, knowing that we would need much more for the upcoming general election.

Little did we know that this would just be the start of the many challenges that would lay ahead as we began to plan for one of the most consequential elections in our lifetimes.

APRIL 2020

IN SEARCH OF GUIDANCE ON HOW TO RUN ELECTIONS IN A PANDEMIC

Before the general election in November 2020, Orange County had to conduct two other special elections in April and May 2020. Despite the uncertainty, our office knew we had to begin planning immediately. If not, we'd miss key deadlines for hiring and training election workers and preparing equipment and supplies for Vote Centers. Yet, there were no guidelines on how to administer an election during a pandemic. "Normal" operations would undoubtedly violate COVID-19 health and safety guidelines.

I felt uneasy and we did our best to continue moving forward with our improvised election plans until we were told otherwise. Neal engaged in conversations with the Governor's office, the Secretary of State's office, and the California Association of Clerks and Election Officials (CACEO) to get clarification. Orange County was not the only office that had to run special elections before the general election.

The Governor's office asked CACEO to share its expertise on what guidelines would be helpful, and Neal was asked by his fellow election official colleagues to put one together; in turn, I was then asked by Neal to prepare a draft for his review. While working on the draft executive order, I felt like the entire situation was surreal. There weren't any established rules or protocols on how to conduct an election in a pandemic.

Then, Governor Gavin Newsom issued Executive Order N-34-20, declaring that election offices would remain open as being part of critical infrastructure. He also signed a waiver to exempt in-person voting for special elections leading up to the general election. I felt relieved, knowing that we would not have to jeopardize the health of our staff and election workers before we could reevaluate all operations to determine how to accomplish what needed to be done safely, transparently, and securely.

The executive order also extended the post-election canvass period. Typically, election offices have up to thirty days after Election Day to complete all post-election audits and ballot processing to officially provide final election results. Any election official worth their salt will always denote that results prior to certification are *un*official results, with a heavy emphasis on the *un* part, so people know that these are not the official results. Media and campaigns like to "call" an election prior to certification; however, that comes with a risk that the candidate with the most votes may change, depending on the number of remaining ballots to count.

Orange County moved swiftly to process ballots and complete post-election audits, so we didn't need the extra time. We were one of the first counties in California to finalize election results for the March 3, 2020 Presidential Primary Election, and it felt good. We had no major issues despite having a 50.1% voter turnout, the highest in a presidential primary election since 2000. On top of that, the high voter turnout and swift election results proved that our transition to Vote Centers and the new voting equipment was a success.

MY ROLE IN THE OFFICE
AND LIFE OUTSIDE OF THE OFFICE

I oversaw one of the largest teams in the office: Outreach, Training, and Community Engagement. Approximately fifty permanent and temporary staff reported to me, and, during the pandemic, they asked questions that I was unfortunately unprepared to answer. In particular, the Community Engagement staff's questions were the most difficult to provide an answer for. This group was the most impacted by the changes caused by COVID-19, as they were the team responsible for educating voters at in-person community events and providing voting equipment demonstrations. At the time, the future of any in-person activities was up in the air and guidelines seemed to change on a daily basis.

As their supervisor, I felt helpless and unable to advocate for them. The directive from top management was to manage resources efficiently, which essentially meant any temporary workers would be let go once they were no longer needed by the operations. Although it was well known that there would be an inevitable end date for temporary workers, the timing was unfortunate as the news began reporting unprecedented layoffs, record unemployment levels, and decreasing employment opportunities.

Since I continued to go into the OCROV office as an essential worker during the pandemic, my experience was that life hadn't changed much except that we started wearing face masks at work, seating arrangements were changed, and our office was closed to the public. Seeing how my life partner Howie changed during the pandemic showed me what most others were going through.

Around this time, Howie started working from home and his workstation took up our dining table. Although busy election periods always made tending to and enjoying our relationship more difficult for the time being, 2020 proved to be extraordinarily difficult. Despite us living together, Howie would not hear from me or see me for up to sixteen hours at a time and, after returning from work, I would be too mentally and physically drained to be as supportive and caring of a partner as I would have liked to be. I would leave for work before he woke up and come home after he had fallen asleep.

Additionally, the novel stress of knowing that I was being exposed to the general public on a daily basis took an unprecedented toll on our relationship. The most Howie was exposed to were the sparrows that would stop by to enjoy the birdseed we put out, and he would occasionally hear noise from our neighbors. His social life had been decimated, and he didn't even have a shoulder to lean on or another being to confide in for most of the day, as I was so preoccupied with the demands of my job that I could not provide the social interaction he needed at the time. Though largely safe from COVID-19, being alone at home with an absent partner was undoubtedly hard.

We decided to get a betta fish. I say "we" but it was really "me" who got excited at a local pet store and persuaded Howie. As a scientist, he naturally understood that the fish tank needed to be maintained at a certain pH level and took to caring for it. As Howie spent numerous hours, days, and nights alone, his life completely altered by the pandemic, the little fish fluttering about in its water tank unaware of the political turmoil and chaos surrounding COVID-19 was a welcome escape from reality.

2020 WESTMINSTER RECALL SPECIAL ELECTION

Shortly after the March 3, 2020 Presidential Primary Election, there were two more special elections planned in April and May 2020. Planning for an election typically starts six months before Election Day with candidate filing, securing voting locations, printing and delivering election materials, etc. We had already sent election materials out, informing voters where voting locations were so they could go vote in person. However, COVID-19 upended our plans.

Due to the pandemic, all planned voting locations were canceled and we did our best to inform voters. We sent postcards to every voter who lived in Westminster and posted signage on the original locations, all of which were translated, which is especially important as Westminster is home to one of the biggest Vietnamese-speaking populations in the country. Westminster is one of the core cities that make up Little Saigon, a social, economic, and cultural hub of the Vietnamese community in Orange County.

Not only was informing voters a challenge, but we had to pivot our internal operations and planning in record time as well.

- ★ We no longer needed to hire Vote Center Customer Service representatives to staff voting locations.

- ★ We no longer needed to train Vote Center Customer Service representatives.

- ★ We no longer needed internal staff to support Vote Center operations.

- ★ We no longer needed to prepare equipment and materials to be delivered to Vote Centers.

- ★ We no longer needed to coordinate and staff operations for the return of ballots from Vote Centers.

California voters were impacted by the pandemic dissimilarly to many other American voters. In fact, the State of Washington doesn't even have voting locations. Every voter votes by mail in Washington and has been doing so since the 2000s. Washington was unintentionally the best prepared for voting in a pandemic as many of its voters were already accustomed to voting by mail and returning their ballots through the mail or a ballot drop box.

Since all Vote Center locations were closed, the only location that voters could go vote in person was the main office in Santa Ana. Once the campaigns figured that out, the voters began to be bussed in—rain or shine.

I distinctly remember Election Day on April 7, 2020. It was an unusually rainy day for Orange County, and we were yet again challenged to pivot to provide for voters standing outside in the rain waiting to vote. We put up canopies and chairs outside, since many of the voters were seniors who could not stand for long periods of time. It was a reminder that, when people understand the importance of voting and know that they have options, they will find a way to vote.

Some people think that Election Day is the end of the election process. Others would say that's when it starts to get exciting. By no means is Election Day the end in California, at least. In California, a ballot can still be processed and counted seven days after Election Day so long as it was postmarked by Election Day. Meaning, if you drop your ballot off at a mail delivery service (i.e., the United States Postal Service, UPS, FedEx, etc.) by Election Day, it has seven days to travel and be received by the elections office.

Then, the signatures on vote-by-mail ballot envelopes are verified. Those who match are counted immediately, but those with either missing or mismatching signatures are set aside for further action. The elections office sends a letter to voters who have missing signatures on their envelopes for the opportunity to "cure" the situation by returning a form declaring under oath they had voted a ballot and are providing a signature to be connected with their ballot. Those who have mismatching signatures are reviewed by several team members for a solid affirmation from the office and receive a similar form with an opportunity to "cure" as well.

In every election, it is expected that someone will be unhappy with the result. After all, the American voting process is definitive and polarizing; you either cast your ballot for a candidate or you don't. You vote for or against a measure, and the aggregate of those responses is reflected in a tally of votes. In the case of the April 7, 2020 City of Westminster Special Recall Election, one side was unhappy enough with the results that they requested a recount.

MAY 2020

LEARNING TO MANAGE A RECOUNT IN A PANDEMIC

Recounts are rare because certain requirements have to be met. There is no provision in California law to require an "automatic recount" in any election contest. Recounts can be expensive and the request must be submitted within five days of the election being certified (which means finalized in election speak).

We soon realized that there are no guidelines for how to run a recount during a pandemic. Typically, recounts are contentious from both sides as the election's outcome could change. Observers hover above staff who are manually counting the ballots, so close that either person can smell what the other had for lunch or whether they drank coffee or smoked. There was no set guideline for how far an observer had to be from a vote counter, and that often led to staff reporting feeling like they were being intimidated. With COVID-19 restrictions, the physical closeness observers were allowed to enjoy changed. The recount area was cordoned off, and cameras and monitors showing what was happening at the recount tables were available to the public for viewing.

As the recount proved that OCROV had correctly reported the election results, operations began to shift toward preparing for yet another special election. This time, it would be for the recall of a Santa Ana City Council Member on May 19, 2020. We learned a lot from the April 7, 2020 City of Westminster Recall Election and ran the next election much smoother. In addition to having more time to plan, we knew we didn't have to prepare for in-person voting and election worker training. Fewer things to prepare for meant we had more time and resources to focus on what was still needed to conduct the election.

At that point, Orange County was the most experienced elections office in terms of facilitating voting and an election during a pandemic in California (perhaps in the nation or world) because we had conducted two elections and a recount under COVID-19 before June 2020. Although we were glad that both of these special elections and a recount went smoothly, we knew we had more to focus on with the 2020 General Election just around the corner.

EXECUTIVE ORDER N-64-20

On May 8, 2020, Governor Newsom issued Executive Order N-64-20 to send every voter a vote-by-mail ballot for the November 3, 2020 Presidential General Election. Since Orange County had already transitioned to a Vote Center model of voting, this executive order aligned seamlessly with our previously laid plans. In the OCROV's work of modernizing voting and elections by transitioning to Vote Centers, we had unexpectedly prepared for a pandemic.

The Vote Center model offers voters the most options for casting and returning their ballot at their own convenience. In Orange County, ballot drop boxes were already installed and vote-by-mail processing was increased; plus, by the time of this executive order, our office and Orange County voters had experienced a major election with both ballot drop boxes and universal vote-by-mail voting.

Following the executive order, 22 million voters in California's 58 counties would automatically receive a mail-in ballot, of which a significant portion had never received a vote-by-mail ballot. Some counties pushed back on the executive order's requirement as they were unsure if they could scale up their operations in time.

Implementing any form of change on a large scale is intimidating and entails high effort and cost. However, voting is a sacred right and democracy is a pillar of American society. All efforts are worth it to ensure more Americans are heard and their government is held accountable to the will of the people. "Is it worth doing to protect our democracy?" is a question I would often ask myself, and the answer was always yes.

PREPARATIONS FOR THE 2020 GENERAL ELECTION BEGIN

As the OCROV began to prepare for the 2020 General Election, it became clear that the old way of cramming hundreds of temporary election workers, all to be hired and trained in the coming months, into one building would not fit in line with the new pandemic distancing requirements. During off-election periods, the building could accommodate its sixty-five permanent staff even when spaced out according to the recommended six feet of distance between workstations.

Our office ballooned up to four hundred or so workers at its busiest, so Neal engaged the County CEO's office to see if there were any other buildings we could use. Fortunately, our neighboring building had been vacated for a remodel but no work had started yet. It was perfect for our needs, but now came the difficult question: Which team(s) would move over and which would stay in the old building?

We discussed options in a management meeting, but which teams would be subject to relocating seemed predetermined. Admin and Warehouse already had their own separate spaces, so they were ruled out. Candidate and Voter Services needed to stay near the front to help voters at the counter, and Outreach aided these same voters with language assistance. Ultimately, it was the Voter Data Services and Training teams that moved to Building B.

At some point during the hectic month of May 2020, Howie's and my fish passed away and it deeply affected him. Although it may have seemed silly to care so much, the comfort that our little pet brought to Howie was significant and meaningful. Having a living companion in the fish offered an escape from the mundaneness of working at home every day during a pandemic, unsure of when we could safely see family and friends and return to the office again.

I found out about the sad news while I was at work. Knowing how much is expected of managers, I was hesitant to let Neal know what had happened and how I immediately considered going home to comfort Howie. Although I was worried that I would be chastised for asking for unplanned time off or be suspected of trying to play hooky, I ultimately decided that being there for Howie was more important than what anyone thought of me and the reason why I was going home.

I once heard about an election worker whose wife went into labor on Election Day. He questioned whether he'd be allowed to leave work to be there for his first child's birth, despite coworkers telling him that he needed to be there for his wife and newborn no matter what else could be happening at work. It's easy to be caught up in work when there is an endless list of things to do, coworkers and voters who are counting on you, and the steady and unforgiving march toward Election Day. I'm glad to share that he left and was able to be at his wife's side when their child was born.

Around the same time, we began to hear praise for essential

workers. From my perspective, when the pandemic hit, healthcare workers and food-service workers were the ones who were truly on the front lines of protecting society and risking their health (mentally and physically) to do so. Though I was considered an essential worker, I didn't feel like one at the time and felt like an impostor. Continuing to go into the office for work during the pandemic was strange; I felt like not much had really changed for me while everyone else's work and social lives had been upended.

Reports initially suggested things would go back to normal by the summer of 2020. However, by the end of May and the beginning of June, it was clear that cases were on the rise and it was too risky to assume that the 2020 General Election could be conducted under normal conditions. After rumors circulated that the 2020 General Election may or may not be conducted as an all vote-by-mail election, Governor Newsom laid the rumors to rest by issuing Executive Order N-67-20, which confirmed that there would be in-person voting options.

JUNE 2020

CREATING THE COVID-19 ELECTION RESPONSE REPORT

We began evaluating every aspect of election and voting operations and determined which aspects would likely be affected by COVID-19. An internal committee with representatives from different teams was formed and charged with preparing an analysis and recommendations for Neal to make decisions on. It was very taxing on the team as we had just gone through the process of evaluating all changes that needed to be made due to the transition from the polling place model to the Vote Center model. At the same time, this evaluation was also something that we knew we could do and, more importantly, we had to do in order to ensure safe, accessible, and secure voting options.

With representatives from each team, the internal committee acted on behalf of OCROV employees to determine what changes would be necessary for staff to feel safe in the workplace. Most recommendations were implemented, such as providing disposable face masks, hand sanitizer, automatic doors, gloves, and tissues. Although there was a desire for plexiglass barriers, the rest of the world wanted them too, so they were impossible to get and super expensive as well.

In addition to providing more health and safety supplies onsite, staff brought up an interest in working remotely. Prior to COVID-19, only managers could work remotely and that was so managers could continue to work after normal work hours, weekends, holidays, and even on vacation and sick days. Now that we were in a global pandemic and official guidance recommending all workers that could work remotely to do so, it was a completely different conversation.

While some employees were able to work remotely, it was clear that other employees could not. For example, those responsible for processing voter registration forms could not take the forms home to complete data entry, and those responsible for the maintenance of voting equipment needed to be onsite in the Warehouse to tend to the machines. As we began to go through each position and department's role and responsibilities, it started to sink in more and more that we were truly essential workers.

After making all these changes, Neal asked me to help prepare an anonymous employee survey, which included these types of questions:

★ How would you rate the agency's communication regarding COVID-19 to date?

★ How would you rate the County's communication regarding COVID-19 to date?

★ Do you have a schedule that works with your circumstances?

★ Do you feel you have adequate access to sanitizing products in the office?

★ How would you rate your overall feeling toward the working environment given the COVID-19 concerns?

☆ Do you feel that you have the tools necessary to complete your daily tasks?

Generally speaking, staff responded positively to these questions; though, you could still sense an undercurrent of worry around the unfamiliar and incessant reminder that the threat and our understanding of COVID-19 was constantly evolving. We sensed that there was no guarantee that the health and safety guidance provided today would be the same as tomorrow.

Once we affirmed that staff felt comfortable about their workplace, we started an internal committee to evaluate all aspects of in-person voting and what would need to change in order to comply with COVID-19 health and safety standards. Several states had their primary election after California in March and April, when the least was known about COVID-19 and officials still urged elections to take place.

You may remember the long lines of voters waiting to vote in person as many states still limited who were able to vote by mail, despite being in a pandemic. I couldn't believe how state representatives were forcing election officials to move forward with conducting an election in person when public health guidance heavily pushed stay-at-home messaging. I felt fortunate to live in California, where we did not have to choose between voting and staying safe during a time of much uncertainty.

With no guidance from the state or federal level, the Orange County Registrar of Voters' COVID-19 Election Response Report would serve as a playbook for many other election offices who also found themselves wanting to prepare for the possibility that election administration would look very different in November 2020. It is no exaggeration that hundreds, if not thousands, of state and local election officials called Orange County asking what we planned to do. The report is still available online at ocvote.com/covid and provides detailed information on changes made, such as:

- ★ Offering online candidate filing

- ★ Increasing internal capacity to handle anticipated historic vote-by-mail usage

- ★ Creating online election worker training

- ★ Debuting the Vote Center Lab, a test environment for election workers to practice processing voters and setting up and breaking down equipment. We also utilized the Vote Center Lab to test out physical distancing measures, develop the ideal setup for an in-person voting location, and conduct tests to determine how long voters would wait if there were fewer voting machines.

- ★ Increasing services for voters with disabilities and voters needing language assistance

- ★ Modifying the post-election audits process

- ★ Planning for observers to safely view virtually and at a distance in-person

- ★ Detailed plans for voter outreach and education

ELECTION OFFICIALS: ESSENTIAL BUT NOT INVINCIBLE

As these changes were happening, it became very evident that, despite our essential and critical mission to prepare for the 2020 General Election, we election workers were every bit affected by COVID-19 as anyone else. We began to notice extended absences by staff. However, the notification and contract-tracing processes were still in development. Since COVID-19 status was related to an employee's health, we couldn't publicly share which employees were out of the office due to COVID-19 despite serious concerns around exposure and wanting to protect ourselves.

No absence was felt greater than that of Neal's. After a few days of not being in the office, staff grew concerned that his reason for being absent was more serious. Then, Neal sent out an office-wide email confirming that, despite taking extra measures to be safe, he had indeed contracted COVID-19. He had asked staff to maintain the confidentiality of his COVID-19 status, and it felt like the weight of his responsibilities had shifted over to us staff, especially the managers.

I truly believe that because Neal experienced COVID-19 early on, he understood the seriousness of the virus and directed resources and staff to prepare accordingly through strict protocols and stockpiling PPE as early as possible.

The challenge of election officials educating voters and pivoting operations in a COVID-19 environment became more and more evident as the pandemic wore on. Fortunately, private and public funding opportunities suddenly became available. I worked closely with our Administrative team to develop grant applications, which received millions of dollars to help with offsetting costs related to supplies, equipment, and outreach to voters.

As the fifth largest voting jurisdiction in the United States, we knew we would experience heavy scrutiny by the public and media in a contentious political environment with millions of dollars poured into divisive campaigns. We were going to prepare for voting in a pandemic, and I was so proud to be part of a team that was deeply committed to ensuring access to voting, transparency, and that the election would be conducted freely, fairly, and securely.

One of my critical team members fell ill to COVID-19 in June 2020 and I was at a loss, as the manager overseeing several teams. I wanted to do everything in my power to support her, but there was not much I could do besides coordinating with Admin. I wanted her to rest and to assure her that the rest was a protected time for her to recuperate and heal.

JULY 2020

DEVELOPING ELECTION WORKER TRAINING UNDER COVID-19

When this team member became ill, she was working on updating election worker training materials. Not only did we need to update the training manual, but we also needed to create online training and refilm training videos. I stepped in to help with the training team to work on these materials, and I felt very fortunate to work with a team just as committed as I was. There was also a lot of pressure as preparing election worker training is relatively early in the in-person planning process and other teams would be waiting for election worker training to be finalized.

Fortunately, the training plan had been approved with this critical team member's input mostly done so we knew what we needed to accomplish and by when. Neal had a very clear vision of where he wanted to have the videos filmed and by whom. He wanted the videos to be filmed at the University Hills Community Center in Irvine, which is affiliated with the UC Irvine campus. This prestigious section of the campus is where many professors and other high-ranking administrators lived with their families. We had previously filmed there so I had a connection with the Irvine Campus Housing Authority's (ICHA) facilities team.

When I reached out to ICHA, there was naturally some hesitation, which I expected. ICHA had closed the University Hills Community Center to all activities regardless of whether they were requested by residents or outside entities. Despite this initial challenge, Neal was undeterred and challenged me to continue looking for ways to secure the filming location. The OCROV eventually succeeded by working with UC Irvine's Community & Government Relations team and ICHA's CEO to ensure we had access to the property and buildings needed for filming.

In addition to the election worker training videos, Neal wanted to create videos that informed voters of their voting options. Completing these videos would include filming at a residential home, at an office, and at a ballot drop box to demonstrate to voters the ease and simplicity of voting at home and returning a ballot.

Looking back, the pressure was overwhelming, knowing we needed to accomplish so much in a short amount of time and that we needed the smooth cooperation of outside agencies in order for us to move forward with preparing election worker training and voter education. Throughout this process, I came to adopt the mindset that nothing is impossible and anything can be accomplished with enough grit, motivation, and connections. Protecting democracy and ensuring voter access was worth overcoming any and all obstacles.

OCROV partnered with an Emmy-nominated production company on videos that informed Orange County voters on the transition to the Vote Center model the year prior, so we had a good working relationship to start with. Somehow, Neal was able to convince this company to assist with the filming and finding a film crew. We started reviewing the State of California's requirements for filming in a COVID-19 environment, and these rules were very stringent. Any film production required a health and safety officer to be onsite at all times to ensure that any person coming onto the set had tested negative for COVID-19 within the days leading up to production and to complete an attestation that they were not experiencing COVID-19 symptoms, had not traveled internationally in the last two weeks, and had not been exposed to someone who had tested positive for COVID-19.

This strict requirement made it very difficult for our agency to balance staffing needs for filming and to continue working on other projects in the office. Only a limited number of staff could be excused to be onsite for filming and had the unenvious challenge of securing COVID-19 testing appointments and results within a week when COVID-19 tests were rare and could only be administered by medical personnel. Although this project brought new uncertainties and risks to our work, I am really proud that many of my staff volunteered to assist with this endeavor.

Ultimately, I was permitted to bring only one other team member to help with filming. As I had more experience with Neal's overall vision and style, I needed help from someone who was well-versed in the technical aspects of election worker training. Even though we had to work offsite to film footage for training videos, I continued to manage my other teams from afar with emails, phone calls, and texts to ensure that we would still be making progress for outreach, translations, media, social media, and pop-up mobile voting.

In addition to being onsite to ensure that filming would go as planned, we needed staff from the Warehouse team to help us bring all of the voting equipment from our office in Santa Ana. Normally, a Vote Center is set up by a team of 6-8 election workers in a few hours, but, due to the COVID-19 restrictions, we could only allow three people to help. It was unbelievably tiring to lift and assemble voting equipment with a smaller team, but we knew we needed to shoulder it; there were no others whom the office could send or were allowed to take our place.

Though we had filmed for only three days, each day included at least twelve hours of filming. While the film crew was as supportive as could be, the responsibility for ensuring the actors' presence and performance, the conduciveness of the set, and the technical accuracy of what was being filmed fell on the shoulders of my team member and myself. We moved and reconfigured all parts of the set without assistance from the film crew, and we would work out voter-processing scenarios as filming was happening in some instances. We were physically and mentally exhausted by the end.

The film crew was also tired. I learned that some of the film crew had previously been involved in major productions in the Marvel Comic Universe and other Hollywood franchises. They said that filming with us was even more tiring than other projects they had worked on, because we didn't take any breaks and we needed lots of close-up and wide shots in various parts of the room, which meant a lot of set-ups and breakdowns. Normally, they'd film only a few scenes in a day on other projects; with us, they were filming over thirty scenes in a day due to our time constraints.

After filming was completed, we now needed to translate and create audio voiceovers in the languages Orange County was responsible for supporting: Spanish, Vietnamese, Chinese, Korean, Gujarati, Hindi, Japanese, Tagalog, and Farsi/Persian. The internal team was able to complete the translations and audio voiceovers within a week, so we could start sending out links to the translated videos to community groups, organizations, and advocates to start educating voters with limited English proficiency about changes to voting and elections due to COVID-19 before ballots were mailed out.

The toil, stress, and exhaustion were all worth it, though. We were able to create a complete election worker training video that met COVID-19 health and safety standards, which no other election office in the entire United States had created yet. Other election offices were waiting for our training video's completion to learn what Orange County was doing differently and to see what they could incorporate from our materials into their training resources. One county, which shall not be named, said that they'd asked if one of their staff members was prepared to do a voiceover of our training video (jokingly—or not), although it would be apparent that the training video originated from Orange County with its obvious branding on all equipment and materials. That felt like a nice compliment for the hard work we put into it.

Orange County's 2020 election worker training video and informational videos can still be viewed online on YouTube at https://www.youtube.com/user/ocrov.

THE REGISTRAR RETURNS

Fortunately, Neal recovered around the time that the videos were finalized and he resumed his normal duties, which included media interviews. He had a strong reputation among news media for his willingness to speak on his experience as an election official and providing access to our facilities and processes for news cameras. Even though it would wear on staff to work with media and be pulled away from our other duties, it was done to highlight our transparency and integrity.

One of my most memorable moments while working at the Orange County Registrar of Voters happened on Election Night of the 2018 General Election. We had just finished processing all of the ballots and equipment that had been returned to our office after polls closed around 3 a.m. the morning after Election Day.

As most staff were walking out of the office, Neal turned around to let a news media crew in to do an "early shot" for a news organization that would go on air for a morning show on the East Coast. I was in awe of the relentless dedication to providing transparency and access, even after a long day and night of the challenges that come with administering a major election for approximately 2 million voters.

In one of the many interviews Neal participated in, he casually shared in a media interview that he had recovered from testing positive for COVID-19 and explained how that impacted the election planning process. We started hearing about other election officials who had also tested positive for COVID-19, and it exemplified how the virus could completely throw off the best-laid plans no matter how well we tried to prepare for whatever could happen.

CANDIDATE FILING
AND TRANSLATIONS BEGIN

Around July 2020, candidate filing was in full swing and our office needed to begin preparing for translating election materials. This meant hiring temporary election aides to assist with translations and proofing in the four federally supported languages: Spanish, Vietnamese, Chinese, and Korean. Fortunately, we had some election aides for Spanish, Korean, and Chinese who had previously worked at our office and were returning to help in this election. Despite this circumstance, we were still severely short of needed assistance and still needed to hire more. The Administrative team was able to find good candidates, whom we hired to fill our staffing needs; however, one election aide left in the middle of the proofing process and we had to fill the position with another candidate. Although I can't fault someone for leaving for a better opportunity, it still made things difficult for the team.

Any person who has worked as either a translator or a translation project manager knows the pain of having to wait for the source file to be finalized before being able to begin work. Starting before the source file is finalized risks missing changes and dealing with version control issues. Yet, when involved with translation work in an environment that is highly deadline-driven like an elections office, it sometimes seems like there is no choice but to begin translating preemptively when you consider the varying deadlines for the external vendors to complete the initial translation, printing deadline, and mailing deadline.

On top of that, you want to get the translations out to the voters at the earliest possibility so that they have enough time to review election materials to cast their ballot as an informed voter. It's already an enormous lift during a regular election cycle, and during the health crisis, the stress was compounded.

There are a few dedicated individuals who feel the weight of being responsible for providing accurate and culturally appropriate translations for their entire community. In Orange County, we are fortunate to have dedicated in-house staff who have institutional knowledge and can train the temporary election aides. The well-being of every employee is important to the operation; however, the absence of those with more responsibilities is more deeply felt and more difficult to fill in.

COVID-19 health and safety guidelines at the time required any individual exposed to COVID-19, experiencing symptoms, or having tested positive for COVID-19 to quarantine for at least ten days and only return to the office after being medically cleared with a negative test or by a doctor. At that time, COVID-19 testing was hard to come by; you had to schedule your test several days out in advance, and it was common to travel to neighboring counties to testing sites with availability. That is to say, even if you experienced just one or a few of the wide range of symptoms (chills, cough, sore throat, etc.), you were out for at least ten days.

As a manager, I greatly cared (and still care) about my team's health, yet I struggled with the realization that the entire translation project could be upended if one of my critical team members was out for that long of a period. It's not like you can cross-train when it comes to translating; translating election materials is a highly valuable skill, and being able to do it under so much pressure and a tight timeline made it even more difficult to find someone who could temporarily fill this role. We weren't even sure we would receive approval to have a temporary replacement. In fact, the lack of funding for election administration means that most (if not all) election offices are understaffed and most staff carry the responsibilities intended for multiple roles. As I looked at my entire team, I realized that the extended absence of any person during the election's most critical times would be absolutely devastating.

Then, the impossible happened. One of my critical team members did not come into the office one day and I received the news: They were experiencing symptoms and had scheduled an appointment to be tested for COVID-19. It was positive, and materials were being approved in English and sent over to my team for immediate translation. This was a huge problem that could undo all of the planning we had prepared. In order to print ballots and prepare voting equipment with electronic and audio ballots, all languages had to finish at the same time.

I always felt extremely anxious about the possibility of not being able to complete translations in the required timeline and, now, it was a very real possibility. The thought of not being able to produce legally required translated election materials affected me deeply; I cared about what it meant for me in terms of my professional abilities, being able to lead my team, and the possible delay of translated election materials, which would negatively impact the voting experience of a segment of voters that already struggled to participate in a democratic process in a language other than their preferred language. In Orange County, approximately 125,000 voters request election and voting materials in another language.

Yet, there was very little I could do. I notified Neal of how the absence of this particular individual and not knowing what the future held could completely derail our plans. I asked him pre-emptively if we could start looking for a temporary replacement to at least keep the project going while this team member was out.

There was a candidate we had initially overlooked for our missing team member's position during the recruitment process who happened to go on to work for the Administrative team. After much pleading and stressing about how difficult it would be to find another candidate to the Administrative Services manager, I worked out an agreement to temporarily "loan" this employee to help with translations either until the translations project was completed or the critical team member recovered and returned. With limited staffing, it's understandable that managers are protective of their staff. However, election administration is a team effort: Even if one team does well, it's imperative all teams are supportive of each other for the overall office to do well.

I breathed a sigh of relief. There was one less thing to worry about now, but plenty of other issues still needed my attention. As election material translations were underway, I shifted my focus to election worker training. With every process and procedure needing to change to reflect new health and safety protocols under COVID-19 and pivoting to a hybrid training including online and in-person training, our election worker training required a complete overhaul in less than eight weeks.

AUGUST 2020

LAUNCHING ONLINE TRAINING UNDER COVID-19

The Orange County Registrar of Voters had historically used an outdated online training platform to train its election workers. The system was very old, clunky, and inefficient. Prior to the pandemic, we were very excited to do away with this outdated online training platform after the 2020 Primary Election. Previously, we had moved or planned to move all election worker training to being in-person since all non-staff election workers, whether they were veteran election workers or working with us for the first time, had not interacted with the equipment and did not know how to utilize the equipment to process voters.

Now, the OCROV was suddenly in this chaotic rush to secure a new online training platform, learn how to use it, create the training content, enroll election workers, and monitor their progress. OCROV was very fortunate to have a strong IT team at the time. Unfazed by unexpected incidents and glitches, the IT team worked very closely with the training team to find a user-friendly solution for both Training staff and election workers who would be taking the training.

Our team felt so lucky that we were able to find a solution with one of the most widely known and used software suites. We immediately began to work on a proposal to gain Neal's approval and work with the Administrative Services manager to get a price estimate on our request. The pricing was based on a number of licenses that were active for a year. It was more realistic to plan with a ballpark number, but it was still challenging to estimate how many people would drop out, whether for being sick or no longer being comfortable in a role that interacted extensively with the public. Interacting with the public could mean interacting with COVID-positive members of the public and/or those who wanted to make a political statement by going to the polls without a mask. Per guidance issued by the Secretary of State, election officials could not prohibit a voter from entering a voting location or casting their ballot based on the voter not wearing a mask.

We eventually settled on a number with an additional percentage set aside for any attrition and completed our proposal. Neal asked a few questions, but he understood that the time constraints our office was under left little leeway for more frugal and otherwise more ideal solutions; the proposal was approved and we began working with the supplier to start onboarding our team.

The work that followed was a bit of a mad rush. We were constantly testing processes, asking other teams to confirm that this was the correct process and that it did not cause other issues downstream, troubleshooting issues as they came up, and then creating content to match what we had learned and confirmed along the way. Then, we had to test the online training platform. We needed testers, but everyone else in the office was busy. That's how things get in an elections office; there are lots of moving parts that need to happen at the same time in order for the election to be conducted properly, timely, securely, transparently, and with integrity. However, that means that workers can often be short on available collaborators.

Thankfully, people graciously made time to ensure that our new training was adequate, and every member of the training team tested the online training portion. I went through some modules as well. Some managers prefer to delegate tasks, which can be the more efficient tactic in some cases, but I enjoyed being hands-on where I could. I always wanted my team to feel like I was working alongside them toward the same goals and cared deeply about what they needed in order to complete their responsibilities and also maintain their well-being.

Once we got to a point where we felt good about the online training (also partially because there simply wasn't more time), we officially launched our online training and election workers began taking the first part of their election worker training for the 2020 General Election. Although we continued to receive feedback on glitches and it wasn't a perfect solution, it was nothing short of a miracle that the Training team had been able to construct the training on such a short timeline and to such a respectable quality. Approximately 1,500 election workers representing the diversity of Orange County's voters would take this training and be prepared to safely and adequately serve voters.

As I think of the dedication, creativity, and hard work required to implement a new training system, I am so deeply proud of my team for their ingenuity, resilience, and unrelenting commitment to helping election workers and voters.

It was made even more evident for me that what is necessary to conduct a successful election cannot be attributed to one person.

Though I recognize the importance of having a good leader, a good leader needs a good team. When I heard that my critical team member who provided many of our translations had recovered and was going to return to the office, I was overjoyed that their health had improved. We briefed this individual on what happened while they were absent, and they picked their work back up as if no time had been lost over the previous few weeks.

IF HEALTH IS WEALTH,
THEN I WAS POOR IN 2020

received an unexpected lesson in mortality shortly after the success of gaining our team member back. I had a bad tendency of forcing myself to stay seated in my desk chair until I would finish a report, presentation, etc. It was my unhealthy way to stop myself from succumbing to any urge to do something else for the sake of productivity. I would bar myself from a variety of activities during my "focus time," whether that be a welcome distraction from work from a coworker stopping by for a chat or an actual need like stretching or eating. It was common for my weight to fluctuate during busy election seasons by about twenty pounds.

One morning, I distinctly remember feeling pain in my left hip as I woke up. As with most annoyances, I tried to brush it off so I could focus on what I thought was more important: getting through the day at work; being present and prepared for my meetings; keeping the peace with the media, public, candidates, and political parties; and motivating my team members even if I was not feeling my best. Election Day was fast approaching, and we were running out of time to prepare for it. Soon, I would learn that this time was different.

At 8 a.m. it was just a little pain. Even at 9 a.m. it was okay. But at 10 a.m. it was *not*. The pain came over me with a vengeance. Years (maybe even decades) of carrying along my day in a sedentary seated position and not stretching enough finally caught up to me. My back muscles spasmed and I could not focus due to the excruciating pain. I sent an email to Neal letting him know that I was dealing with a personal emergency and needed to leave immediately.

Howie was working from home at the time and he was very surprised to see me come home early. Since I don't like to bring attention to my own inconveniences, he was probably even more surprised to hear me exclaim that my hip felt like it was going to fall off and that I needed medical assistance to figure out what was going on.

I was very fortunate to have never experienced a "serious" condition prior to this. I have never suffered a broken bone, fracture, surgery, etc. I also consider myself to have a strong pain tolerance; when getting my first tattoo on my ribcage, the tattoo artist said he would give me a twenty-dollar discount if I stayed quiet during the session. I stayed so quiet that he thought I had fallen asleep! In actuality, I was just determined to save some money as a recent college graduate working at my first big-girl job and I didn't want to play into the stereotype that women cannot handle pain. After that experience, I reconsidered how high my pain tolerance was.

After contacting my primary care physician's office and my healthcare provider, it became very clear that I could not see a doctor right away. Hospitals were overburdened with fewer staff to help those needing routine healthcare services and those dealing with COVID-19. In-person appointments were limited to those who had preplanned appointments or serious situations needing immediate attention. Even those who had tested positive for COVID-19 were told to stay at home unless it progressed to a life-or-death situation.

I didn't want to go to urgent care so I settled for a telehealth virtual appointment. Howie was so sweet to support me during the appointment. I was in so much pain that I had to lie down in order to minimize the pain.

The doctor asked me to walk on camera, which I performed to the best of my ability. I stumbled while wrapping myself with the bedsheet and limped back to bed, relieved to be lying down again. He said it was too hard to tell what my condition was so he recommended I schedule an in-person appointment with a doctor so they could analyze my condition. I'd have to endure more waiting time before experiencing actual relief, unfortunately.

In the days that I waited to meet with my doctor, I would wake up with excruciating pain in the lower back and hip area. It was so bad that I had to sleep in another room since I would scream upon waking up. Howie was concerned by my condition but did not like the screaming one bit, so I think refraining from sharing a bed with him during the time was the right decision. When I would wake up with this incredible pain, I would draw a hot bath and that would be the only time my body would relax and the spasms would dissipate.

By the time I met with my doctor, some of the pain had started to dissipate, but it would often reemerge with a vengeance whenever I would stretch the wrong way or sit for too long. At my appointment, my doctor prescribed muscle relaxers and physical therapy. My doctor told me that the condition I was experiencing was atypical for someone my age and usually experienced by someone in their forties and fifties. It was depressing to hear that my body's age was much older than my actual age of thirty at the time.

I was hesitant to use the muscle relaxers and resolved to utilize the physical therapy solution to recover. I was fortunate to have amazing physical therapists look after me and guide me to recovery. I had to start slowly, as even raising my legs straight into the air was painful; it was hard to face as I used to pride myself on being flexible. After not taking care of myself, I knew I had to start my physical therapy from scratch, no matter how painful or embarrassing it was.

I was lucky to come back from this hip injury successfully. At one point, the pain felt so excruciating that I thought I would willingly amputate my leg if it meant that the pain would stop. I wish I could reach out to my younger self and let her know that taking five minutes away from the desk to walk, stretch, or use the restroom would not have negatively impacted my work and that my health was worth the loss of five minutes of focus. How I wish I could go back in time.

Knowing I would be out of the office for some time, I began feeling the pressure and the guilt. I had over two hundred hours of sick time saved up, but calling out sick when we had so much to do seemed unthinkable. When I gave Neal my doctor's note about having to take time off for three physical therapy sessions a week, I'm sure the thought of how my absence could impact operations and planning crossed his mind. I know I worried about my critical team member being out for COVID-19 and what it would mean for the rest of us. We were stretched so thin and there weren't that many staff to begin with.

I was surprised to see Neal's calm response. "Schedule them whenever it works best for you."

MODIFIED ELECTION ADMINISTRATION WAIVER

Around this time, the Secretary of State's office began sending out questionnaires to county election officials to understand how elections would be conducted in each county. Many counties had been waiting for guidance from the Secretary of State's office, but by August, it was much too late. If the OCROV had waited until July or August to begin planning for a major election in November, we would have been in big trouble.

The Secretary of State created an application for counties to submit a waiver request so that counties could conduct elections that offered fewer services than a normal election. This waiver was being offered to accommodate counties that had trouble recruiting election workers, voting locations, scaling operations, etc. Orange County was actually planning to do the opposite: As a result of the pandemic making voting more difficult, we wanted to go above and beyond what was required to administer elections.

This crisis was also an opportunity for counties that wanted to pilot a different model of voting. Largely, voting hasn't changed in the United States since the 1800s. Election Day has been on

Tuesdays because that used to be the day that most people came into town to do their shopping from their farms. We know that narrative is completely outdated now, given how society, the economy, and technology have changed.

In reality, the day that would be most convenient for the vast majority of American voters would be a Saturday or Sunday since many people don't have work then. Some have claimed that keeping Election Day on Tuesday is desirable because it maintains tradition, but my opinion is that it's just a guise to limit voting access, especially when voters have difficulty accessing or have no access to voting by mail.

At last, I received a response from the Secretary of State. We learned Orange County didn't need a waiver at all because the waiver notification and approval was only needed if we planned to provide a *lower* level of service to voters. Since we were going to provide a higher level of service, voters might be surprised (but in a good way) that they would have even more options, and we affirmed we would be notifying voters about how voting and elections would be conducted in Orange County for this particular election.

NOTIFYING THE PUBLIC ABOUT VOTING UNDER COVID-19

*N*ow that election worker training and translation of election materials were well underway, I shifted my focus to planning pop-up mobile voting and workshops. Although we were excused from having to receive a waiver for how we'd conduct the 2020 General Election, the OCROV was still required to host several public workshops to provide additional voter outreach and education, and in particular languages designated by federal law.

There was one positive in conducting voter outreach through the pandemic: the rise and familiarity of virtual meetings and presentations. With the ability for all with access to the internet to attend our workshops, we saw a huge increase in our voter education workshop attendance in comparison to the in-person workshops we conducted in advance of the 2020 Primary Election. If I recall correctly, the 2020 General workshop for the Chinese community had over seventy attendees whereas the 2020 Primary workshop for the Chinese community had just a fraction of that attendance. As a best practice, I would recommend a hybrid approach to serve both folks who enjoy in-person interactions and those for whom virtual presentations may be more convenient.

PLANNING POP-UP MOBILE VOTING

At the same time that I was overseeing how our voter education workshops were being planned, I was also in charge of planning our pop-up mobile voting operations as well. In an effort to make these location selections less political, the OCROV identified one pop-up mobile voting location per supervisorial district in the county. Our office received recommendations from the community and would compare those recommendations to existing Vote Center locations. The idea is to use pop-up locations to fill in the gaps of where we have our Vote Centers that are open for ten days and four days leading up to election day.

Planning pop-up voting was always a challenge. Neal would have certain areas he'd want to focus on and we'd have to try to convince the property owners to allow us to take a large portion of their property or parking lot for us to set up. Now that I had the experience of a few election cycles, I knew to schedule pop-up mobile voting with a day in between to serve as a break for the staff.

Typically, the temporary staff hired for the Community Engagement team would transition over to assist with pop-up voting. However, Neal provided direction to not hire a Community Engagement team since no events were being held in-person leading up to the 2020 General Election. As a result, I needed to procure staffing for the pop-up voting team from the existing team. This was a very delicate dance with the other teams and especially the managers.

I was very fortunate to have a good working relationship with all the managers. Since I oversaw different teams, I interacted with all teams and made it a point to maintain good relations with everyone. It was not the first time this election cycle that I needed to "borrow" an election aide from another team either. It can get quite contentious at times with managers when their direct reports are reporting to another manager. Favorability and trust go a long way in any group dynamic.

OCROV invested in a large mobile pop-up mobile voting unit that looks a lot like the commercial pop-up stores that you see in retail settings and has been repurposed to offer voting opportunities. However, there's very little about it that actually pops up. The time that it takes to set it up actually is about two hours at minimum, and that's with trained staff who are familiar with setting up the unit and also voting equipment. Another challenge for the pop-up voting team is working together in a way that is most streamlined and efficient. Since the location changes every day, the team has to repeat voting equipment setup that the regular election workers only have to do once.

In addition to identifying staff for the pop-up voting team, I was responsible for securing locations that would allow OCROV to host its mobile pop-up voting unit for an extended period of time. I primarily was looking for spaces with large parking lots that I could take over a portion of to set up our unit and designate parking spots for voters and that had storage for additional voting equipment and materials. Working with property owners and property managers could be a headache, due to worries around liability, loss of parking spots for their stores and customers, and being associated with voting and elections—even though our office is nonpartisan.

We appealed to their sense of civic duty, and we countered their concerns about loss of business by saying that voters coming to vote would increase traffic at neighboring businesses. Sometimes, we intentionally sought out property owned by public agencies as they were easier to work with. Pop-up mobile voting could start as soon as ballots were mailed out, which is twenty-nine days before Election Day. When pop-up voting would be scheduled before ten-day Vote Centers were open, we would either stick to an 8 a.m. to 5 p.m. schedule or whatever time range was allotted by the property manager. Keep in mind, although operating hours were 8 a.m. to 5 p.m., setup would begin at 5 a.m. and breakdown would (hopefully) end by 7 p.m. There was always the possibility that breakdown could be delayed if a voter was still in the process of voting.

By state law, we could not shut down voting operations until the last voter who was in line by closing time had finished voting. Whether that meant thirty minutes after or hours after closing time, it did not matter. Voting locations had to stay open for the last voter to finish casting their ballot. If they complained later on because of how late the pop-up voting ran, I'd refer to the statute requiring our operations to stay open and apologize and beg for forgiveness later. As challenging as it was, the pop-up mobile voting operations were all being done in order to provide the most accessibility and service to voters. Having a positive voter experience was of utmost importance to us.

"HOW IS ORANGE COUNTY PLANNING TO RUN THE 2020 GENERAL?"

In August 2020, OCROV began to receive calls from other local and state election officials from California and across the country, asking about how Orange County was planning to administer the election while complying with COVID-19 health and safety guidelines. Many of these officials felt lost, nervous, and out of time. The deadline-driven schedule of voting and elections is unforgiving and, no matter how much money, staff, etc. you throw at a problem involved with election administration, you can never have more time. This is why it is so critical to have a well-thought-out plan that involves all aspects of the election and many backup plans (even backup plans for the backup plan).

For me, it felt surreal to speak to state election officials who struggled with outreach to their language communities and weren't prepared for election worker training, even though the election was happening with fewer than ninety days left. Even though Orange County is only one of fifty-eight counties in California, we were more familiar with certain aspects of election administration for a large population. It shouldn't come as a surprise, though; the number of voters in Orange County surpasses the number of voters in numerous states.

OCROV serves approximately 2 million voters, which is more voters than the total voters that the states of Alaska, Vermont, Maine, Rhode Island, North Dakota, Delaware, New Hampshire, West Virginia, South Dakota, New Mexico, Nebraska, Montana, Kansas, Hawaii, Arkansas, Nevada, Utah, Idaho, and Wyoming each serve. According to the California Secretary of State, California serves 22 million voters in total.

OCROV fielded many questions from election officials during this critical time. Whether these questions were related to training election workers, conducting outreach, increasing vote-by-mail ballot processing capacity, online candidate filing, etc., OCROV knew it to be important to take the time to share what we knew, our resources, and our time so that elections could be run as best as possible in other parts of the country.

SEPTEMBER 2020

SPORTING VENUES STEP
UP FOR DEMOCRACY

With many properties closing their doors and operations in response to COVID-19, election offices across the country found it harder and harder to find places willing to serve as a Vote Center. Sporting arenas and concert venues were not immune to the effects of COVID-19 either. Large sites like these meant for massive gatherings were ghost towns with all concerts, sporting games, and special events canceled for the foreseeable future.

As they sat empty, something unexpected but wondrous happened. Professional sporting associations began offering their empty spaces to election offices to serve as mega-voting locations, intended to serve as a central and well-known location for voters to cast their ballot. As this was a novel and promising opportunity, utilizing such a space as a voting location was something OCROV sought out immediately as the announcement was made. We contacted the Honda Center in Anaheim, which is home to the National Hockey League's Anaheim Ducks (as you may be familiar with from Disney's *Mighty Ducks* movie series). Fortunately, the Honda Center was supportive and enthusiastic about partnering with us.

We approached the Honda Center team with two requests: 1) We may utilize the Honda Center as a "Super" Vote Center with drive-thru voting and drive-thru ballot drop-off options, and 2) We may host a press conference with a sneak preview of how voting would look in the 2020 General Election. We experienced some challenges with the Honda Center also being used by the Recorder Clerk's office for civil marriage ceremonies, but we ultimately were able to make it work by shifting some pieces around.

While we had more time to evaluate what the logistics would look like for the Honda Center to actually serve as a Vote Center, we had much less time to convincingly demonstrate to the media and, thus, voters what to expect if they came to vote in-person at a Vote Center.

Yet, the most difficult part was still ahead of us. Staff created a diagram on how to maximize the space. Neal wanted the Vote Center to present as endless rows of voting booths to counter the then-popular narrative that voting would be unsafe and there would not be enough booths for voting when the time came.

At this point, we were less than sixty days away from Election Day and, in order to staff this press conference with so many moving parts, we had to pull staff from other projects to become trained on how to process voters at a Vote Center and through drive-thru voting under the new training guidelines we'd created especially for voting in a pandemic. Looking back on how it all came together, I can appreciate how this press conference truly was an amazing team effort involving Operations, Outreach, Election Services, Warehouse, IT, and Training in order to make it all work.

I hadn't realized how long I had not seen rows of media reporters and photographers until it was the day of the press conference. I imagine that because this was one of the very few in-person press conferences anyone was hosting with lots of photo opportunities, we had very good media coverage.

No other election offices were offering media previews of voting, and the dynamics of the 2020 General Election continued to get more and more controversial as we neared Election Day. Even the mascot for the Anaheim Ducks made an appearance at the press conference and was processed as a voter. The Honda Center team was so enthusiastic about our partnership that they created specialty branded "I Voted" stickers, and I kept one as a memento.

OCROV had the responsibility of demonstrating to voters that no matter how divisive politics were or how harrowingly COVID-19 continued to ravage our communities, NOTHING would prevent a voter from being able to exercise their right to vote. We enlisted the help of the same firm that supported our marketing and communications efforts in the 2020 Primary Election to inform voters of the new voting model. The goal of September 2020's marketing campaign, a multimillion-dollar effort, was to saturate the market with information about voting and elections. You couldn't watch television, commute, or listen to the radio without hearing or seeing something from our office about the upcoming election and how to find more information on OCROV's website.

A RIGHT TO PUBLIC OBSERVATION

As the time neared, we began receiving interest from the Secretary of State and external groups about how OCROV would ensure that the public would have the ability to observe the voting and election process once our staff started to process vote-by-mail ballots and during the in-person voting period. Somehow, OCROV would have to balance the right of the public to observe and the health and safety of election workers who were actively engaged with the process. We were able to do this on a smaller scale during the recount for the Westminster special election in April 2020, but that wouldn't suffice in a major general election, where we could expect to host up to one hundred observers at a time at our facility.

The IT team had some ideas involving multiple large monitors, social distancing floor stickers, and even the option of being able to exercise the right to monitor this process remotely. Remote observation was previously thought to be completely out of the question. Neal conferred with the County's attorneys and the Secretary of State's office for their opinion on how to navigate these uncharted waters in providing remote opportunities to observe the election process during a pandemic.

The result was a bit simplistic in nature, but it did the job. All who were interested in observing remotely would review a legal document with certain responsibilities and restrictions and submit it for processing by the office before they were allowed to observe remotely. Some processes could be viewed virtually and some required being in the office to view. Whether there was more done behind the scenes, like a background check or something similar, I have no idea. For the most part, it worked; we received a few complaints overall, but observers had access, which was the goal.

If you wanted to observe in person, you had to make a reservation online. We received some complaints about the difficulties of using the reservation system. However, I attribute the complaints to many people's confusion and dissatisfaction with vote monitoring requiring an additional step as opposed to how they were previously able to show up at our office whenever they wanted.

At the time of no vaccines, we as staff were wary of opening up our office and warehouse to potentially hundreds, if not thousands, of members of the public who were likely upset about how the election had been portrayed, what candidates had to say about voting and elections, election results, etc.

INCREASING MISINFORMATION AND CONSPIRACY THEORIES

As other county election officials do in California, the Orange County Registrar of Voters would send out postcards notifying voters of changes to their voter record. Sometimes, this was at the request of the voter or it was a flag in the voter database that suggested that they may have moved. These data sources could be from death records, home purchases, lease agreements, etc. OCROV partnered with a third-party vendor to receive this data.

Because of the heightened scrutiny and tension we all felt leading up to the 2020 General Election, a routine procedure our office would do to ensure Orange County's voter rolls were up to date prior to mailing out ballots became controversial. It should come as no surprise that many people moved during 2020 in the days and months after the world began to shut down. People moved because their workplaces and schools closed to prevent the spread of COVID-19. People moved to different cities, states, and sometimes to other countries so that they could take care of their loved ones. Yet, many still weren't sure if this would be a permanent move or how long they would stay in their new home.

Despite the uncertainty, Election Day drew closer and closer and every voter record needed to have a residential address to determine which offices a voter was eligible to vote at and a mailing address, if a voter preferred to have their ballot mailed somewhere other than their residential address.

Due to the pandemic, voting by mail was a natural fit with the "stay at home to save lives" message; one could avoid the crowds and avoid potentially contracting COVID-19 from others at a Vote Center or polling place simply by receiving, voting, and returning their ballot all without having to leave the comfort of their home. Since there were also issues with the U.S. Postal Service supply chain, some voters worried about whether their ballot would return to the elections office.

Any Vote Center or polling place could accept returned ballots, but the limited days and hours of operation could still be a hassle for voters. A packed parking lot where in-person voting is offered on Election Day might cause some voters to feel anxious and some hesitation to come inside. Some election offices offer ballot drop-off locations and some of these locations even offer twenty-four-hour availability, which is extremely convenient for voters.

Despite the convenience and simplicity of the system, paranoia started to take hold on voters and the media thrived on the controversy of ballot drop boxes. Some argued that the ballot drop boxes were not secure enough, although they knew nothing about the integrity and installation of the ballot drop boxes. Each ballot drop box in Orange County is installed directly onto cement, weighs a thousand pounds, and has no exposed bolts on the outside.

Anyone who thinks that it would be easy to steal a ballot drop box would be in for a surprise; removal of a ballot drop box would require intensive tools and a flatbed truck and would cause significant noise and attention. In fact, a media news van hit a ballot drop box at our office in the 2020 Primary Election, and the vehicle incurred more damage in that collision, as OCROV merely had to replace some paint on the ballot drop box and there was no structural damage to it.

One of our greatest fears related to ballot drop boxes did happen, though. To this day, it is still unknown who intentionally ignited a fire inside a ballot drop box in Los Angeles County. Unfortunately, Los Angeles County's ballot drop boxes were not equipped with any mechanism to automatically extinguish a fire, and several dozen ballots were damaged and some were even destroyed.

As an elections official and a passionate participant of democracy, I felt heartbroken about there being no way to know which voters were impacted and needed to be notified. At the time, there was no tracking system to know who had dropped off a ballot until the ballot was retrieved and scanned in the central vote processing office. In response, Orange County piloted a high-tech tool to track a ballot from the moment it was dropped off at a ballot drop box in the 2022 Primary Election.

When asked by voters and concerned advocates about whether ballots in Orange County would be protected against similar arson attempts, OCROV was grateful that we had already considered this possibility and planned for it. Every ballot drop box in Orange County was equipped with an automatic fire suppression unit, and we had tested the units with the Orange County Fire Authority in 2019 in advance of deploying the ballot drop boxes in the 2020 Primary Election. Fortunately, there were no attempts to ignite a fire in a ballot drop box in Orange County in the 2020 General Election. However, there would be plenty of controversies involving ballot drop boxes in Orange County leading up to Election Day.

In addition to unfounded beliefs that vote-by-mail ballots returned through the postal service and ballot drop boxes would not be counted, there was also misinformation that only votes cast in person would be counted. This misinformation encouraged voters to go vote in person regardless of what voting method was most convenient or safest for individual voters. As a result, a significant number of voters were under the spell of misinformation and outrageous claims about the integrity of the voting system.

There were so many conspiracy theories about vote-by-mail ballots that our office created a Frequently Asked Questions (FAQs) page for it. Though our office would remain uninvolved with politics as we were simply in charge of administering the election, there was no doubt that our office was impacted by then-President Donald Trump's unfounded allegations about the lack of security around vote-by-mail ballots, despite it hypocritically being his preferred method of casting a ballot. It is no secret that vote-by-mail ballots make it easier for many people to vote and, in the 2020 General Election, it could be a lifesaving way to vote too. Politicians seeking to eliminate or reduce vote-by-mail voting are suppressing the vote and, unfortunately, we've seen a significant rise in efforts by state legislatures following the 2020 General Election to restrict or eliminate vote-by-mail voting for partisan gain.

Much of the misinformation was and continues to be promoted through social media. Behind the curtain of anonymity and the tendency of social media users to not check for references or proof, conspiracy theories ran the full gamut. Even more challenging,

OCROV knew that misinformation was being spread in other languages through our communities, and we did not have enough staffing resources to be able to monitor social media in multiple languages. Additionally, there were some social media platforms that county government agencies were not allowed to use, and we were not able to see what misinformation was being spread and to address it. The lack of response from our office could serve as the lack of a counter to the online conspiracies, leading some social media users to accept it as fact without any authoritative figure to challenge it.

Despite the limited staffing and limited time, I helped OCROV update its social media toolkit. The Social Media Toolkit was created with other government offices and community organizations in mind to help OCROV amplify its message and information-sharing efforts with the general public.

The Social Media Toolkit provided the following:

- ★ General information about voting options

- ★ Hashtags promoting accessibility, security, and convenience

- ★ Sample social media posts for Facebook, Instagram, and Twitter

- ★ An overview of available digital resources such as informational videos, newsletters, weblinks, radio streaming spots, flyers, brochures, social media images, press releases, and FAQs

- ★ COVID-19-related digital materials

Compiling social media and digital marketing collateral in a single document proved to be very helpful. We saw cities, community organizations, and other groups use the same images and messages OCROV would use in its social media posts. It was empowering to see our efforts reach more audiences than we had solely through OCROV's social media accounts, which created a compounding effect every time someone liked, commented, or reshared the post.

However, digital efforts to get the word out about voting would not be enough. OCROV understood that there are many people who do not use social media and, frankly, it's immensely easy to get lost in the overwhelming amount of ads and posts that are trying to get your attention over social media. To cover our bases, we moved forward on our plans to mail out Vote Center postcards to all 1.6 million voters. Not only would our office provide general voting and election information such as the closest Vote Center and ballot drop box based on their residence address, but we also made plans to change the model on the front of the postcard based on the demographics of the voter's zip code and the language based on the language preference in the voter's record.

I assisted in proofreading the templates and overseeing the translation of the content and knew that my colleagues had a colossal undertaking to analyze voter records data and have it work with the design software. In an elections office, it is clear that every team needs to work together and that each team's objectives likely depend on another team's success, so we are always looking to support one another even if we don't have subject matter expertise.

Another benefit of sending another Vote Center postcard before we mailed out ballots was that it would be another opportunity for voters to update their voter registration record should anything important, like their residence address, need to be changed. That is, of course, assuming they are forwarding their mail or have someone checking their mail for them.

It really felt like democracy and the future of the United States were on the line and we could lose it all if we didn't play our little role in ensuring we conducted the election as best we could and made voting as accessible as possible in the first major election to be conducted during a pandemic in Orange County. In some ways, everything really was on the line and our country had a close call.

WHAT WOULD YOU SACRIFICE FOR DEMOCRACY?

The dedication to our work meant we were sacrificing all of ourselves: sleep, exercise, rest, nutrition, and everything in between. No matter how energetic, talented, or skilled someone is, all humans need rest. I recall how I motivated myself to keep pushing when my body screamed for attention and care, even though I should have listened to my body instead. I would ask myself, "Is it worth sacrificing _____________ to protect democracy?" and the answer was always yes; it was a very dangerous game to play with myself. We were past the stage of burnout at this point, but it felt like we couldn't stop with so many more things to do and prepare for. Unfortunately, that meant we weren't performing at as high of a level that we would normally.

Neal was fed up with all of the small mistakes our team had made and called a special management meeting. In this meeting, it became extremely clear that Neal was not pleased with how things were going, and he ordered a hard stop on all printing and mailing operations. Everyone involved, from the managers to line staff, was impacted and this forced all teams to pause their work and not advance forward. As we were preparing vote-by-mail packets and Vote Center postcards to go out to mail, this caused a massive change to our timeline and all staff were very antsy about it.

Reflecting on it now, it may have been Neal's way of forcing us to rest and showing us that, even under incredible pressure and deadlines, rest was necessary and worth letting other things be delayed if it meant that we could come back refreshed and with a clearer mind. Though the break was small and it made us anxious at the time, we needed the break.

THE RACE TO TRAIN 1,500 ELECTION WORKERS

Leading up to the March 2020 primary, election worker training was held at various sites throughout Orange County. Election workers were required to complete three days of in-person training as opposed to two to three hours of training for volunteer poll workers before the Vote Center transition. With the change to the Vote Center model and new COVID-19 protocols, there was a complete overhaul of the training process for election workers.

As we entered the post-election phase of the March 2020 primary, it was common to reach out to our various facility contacts that provided their space to be utilized as a training space. In our thank you card, we would include an enamel election pin and a thank you message to express our gratitude, and in some instances an inquiry to seek partnership again as a training space for the upcoming general election in November. As we were creating our thank you mailers, the team was instructed to hold off on any mentions of future partnerships as there was uncertainty building from the pandemic.

As planners, we were constantly working to ensure that any work that could be done ahead of time, such as securing training locations, was completed as soon as possible. So this was the first signal for the training team that this pandemic might completely derail our plans that we had so carefully crafted for the Vote Center transition.

Sometime later, it became clear to the team that we would in fact have to completely redevelop our training program for the second time within a span of six months. With the new voting equipment acquired, new procedures were written to instruct election workers how to process voters and how to open and reopen the polls over multiple days of voting.

There was a steep learning curve for those who were used to operating the old voting equipment, but we intentionally designed a learning program that allowed our election workers to have three eight-hour days of hands-on training to fully understand the operation and security of our voting equipment. The pandemic completely changed our plans.

The highly contagious virus recommended against large gatherings and encouraged physical distancing wherever possible. In previous elections, the training classes ranged anywhere from twenty to eighty individuals, depending on the size of the facility, and everyone worked in relatively close proximity to operate the voting equipment. Classes were often divided into small groups to learn how to set up and break down equipment.

We understood the major challenge we were facing. We had to make a training program that would be sufficient to cover the knowledge gaps among our election workers while still being one that would keep them safe during a global pandemic. We adopted a hybrid training program equivalent to three days of training, with two days being completed online at the learner's own pace at home, and one eight-hour day of onsite training.

This was a major shift for many of our teams. For the Training team, they worked rapidly to acquire a learning management system and create interactive online training courses that would cover the essential knowledge needed to operate a Vote Center. This was a challenge on its own, as many of the returning trainers who were knowledgeable in the Vote Center operations were not instructional designers and had to learn a completely new skill set to create the training program.

Additionally, there was still the challenge of creating an in-person training that would be safe for everyone. Instead of moving to an offsite facility, we concluded it would be best to host all our training on our OCROV campus and utilize the Vote Center Lab as best we could. Given the square footage of the Vote Center Lab, we limited the number of in-person classes to twenty people at most. We worked with our Warehouse team to secure enough space in the warehouse to set up large tables for learners to practice on the electronic poll books and open floor space to learn how to set up and break down equipment.

During each day of training, we would invite three classes of twenty students and each class would rotate through the different topic areas of "Voter Processing," "Equipment Set-up / Breakdown," and "Vote Center Simulation." The training area was optimal as it was in a large warehouse and the doors were open for airflow. The perimeter was secured so anyone who was unauthorized would be unable to enter the training area.

The top two challenges were the heat and sound. The high

ceilings, wide space, and open doors did not help with keeping the area cool during the common fall heat waves. To combat this issue, we rented several mobile air conditioning units that could be placed around the training areas and keep the immediate area cool. The environment in the warehouse also posed challenges when it came to sound. The open-air layout meant the sound was more likely to travel and it would be harder to hear. We worked with the IT team to acquire microphones and speakers for the trainers to use in their classes, and we asked surrounding groups and teams to be mindful and avoid causing other loud noises or disturbances.

Soon, election worker training started, and the race to hire and prepare nearly 1,500 temporary election workers, or Vote Center Customer Service representatives (CSRs) as we called them, in time for the 2020 General Election began. Due to the serious health advisories issued for seniors related to COVID-19, many of the older election workers who would regularly work chose not to return for the 2020 General Election.

Many were first-time election workers; their stories represent the wide diversity within our society at all levels. Some had been laid off as a result of the faltering economy, some felt a strong sense of duty in light of the controversial national rhetoric around politics, and some were curious about what happened behind the scenes of an election. Yet, all were committed to ensuring voting access even at great personal sacrifice and threat to their health.

OCROV had recently completed construction of the first-ever Vote Center Lab. Similar to a test restaurant kitchen, the Vote Center Lab was a permanent standing structure in the warehouse to mimic the environment of an actual Vote Center. The Vote Center Lab would utilize the same equipment, setup, and materials of a Vote Center to allow tours for the public and a setting where election workers could practice and gain experience processing voters before the actual voting period. This was tremendously helpful for the office to also evaluate which pieces of election worker training needed to be modified to fit COVID-19 health and safety guidelines; examples include wiping down equipment after each use, providing voters with a disposable pen, and providing election workers with face masks and gloves.

Traditionally, election worker training was held throughout Orange County at various sites and only required 2-3 hours. However, since election workers needed to be trained on a completely new process, the requirement now became three days of eight-hour training onsite at the OCROV office in Santa Ana. Not only was this a massive change for the election workers, it was a big change for all departments on the campus. Parking became an issue and so did bathrooms. Fortunately, there were plans to bring outdoor bathrooms.

After election worker training ended, I recall reading a community opinion piece titled "Poll Workers Doing Their Part for Democracy" in *Voice of OC* by Theresa Keegan, an election worker who shared personal reflections of the election worker training experience. She wrote, "I remembered why democracy is so wondrous… Throughout the day other training groups arrived. It was as if a synchronous dance were being performed throughout the huge elections office warehouse." Her comments moved me, and I felt great pride in the work my team and I had done to ensure this election would be successful.

Hearing unprompted validation from outside, non-affiliated individuals and organizations made us feel like we were doing the right thing when it sometimes felt like we couldn't do enough. Specifically, members of the public who believed the conspiracy theories and lies that had been spread about the integrity of the election actively made it difficult to complete our work to the point where it was almost unbearable.

I refused to break under their pressure, but its toll on me was noticeable. I started to feel more paranoid about being followed home after leaving work or watched, even outside of work. I intensely craved the calmness of a controlled environment when I was not working to balance the chaos I experienced when I was in the office and anytime I responded to work calls and emails.

MAGA TARGET #1: ELECTION OFFICIALS

The unfortunate strategy then-President Trump preemptively took to call into question and invalidate election results if they were not in his favor continues to have major consequences for the American public and democracy itself. Distrust of election officials, who understand voting and election laws and regulations best, grew as we neared Election Day. Members of the public who believed in these conspiracy theories and lies bombarded not only our office but election offices across the country. This negative experience pushed many election officials and staff to leave the field after the 2020 General Election, myself included unfortunately.

In an effort to combat misinformation, our office created the Trusted Election Official Page with answers to commonly asked questions and voting myths. Not only did this help members of the public who were seeking nonpartisan information, but this also helped our office have consistent messaging across the staff assisting at the front counter, public phone bank, etc.

The website contains verified information on several categories: Vote-By-Mail, Registration, Jury Duty, Vote Center, Ballot

Drop Boxes, Remote Accessible Vote-By-Mail Ballots. In essence, almost every part of the operation was called into question, and there needed to be accessible, thorough information (to the point of tedium) about every aspect of the election. When people don't understand something, they distrust it, which is understandable. However, problems arise when they don't try to understand it or don't try to learn more about it, opting instead to consume propaganda from (at best) misinformed or (at worst) malicious sources.

Distrust in the voting and election system and those responsible for its proper operation would cause our entire democracy to crumble if this view was held by a majority or plurality of Americans. It is scary to think about but, given how recent events have caused some to question whether the United States is a functioning democracy, it is a reality that we need to consider as a possibility. Therefore, it was and continues to be key for the government and organizations and individuals who believe in democracy to maintain a dialogue with skeptics and provide accurate, up-to-date information about elections.

As campaigns continued to strategize against each other and conspiracists continued to spread lies, it became evident to others watching from the outside just how poorly equipped election offices were to handle the immense scrutiny, mandated requirements, and tsunami of election deniers and unscrupulous observers. I remember being pleasantly surprised to hear that there was a major funding opportunity for election offices to prepare for the 2020 General Election. Congress didn't allocate more money to help make the general election happen, after an initial allotment during the primaries. That left local election officials desperate for other funding sources.

The Center for Tech and Civic Life (CTCL) announced the availability of millions of dollars specifically for election administrators in September. CTCL also invited every single election department in the entire country to apply for grant funding if they needed it and funded every application that came in. Since there was minimal or no additional funding for election offices to now figure out how to administer elections despite the additional challenges caused by COVID-19, this was most welcome news and honestly likely played a significant role in protecting the integrity of elections conducted for the 2020 General Election in the United States. Orange County received a few million dollars from CTCL, which was a significant new pool of funds to support health and safety supplies, voter outreach and education, improved processing, and increased salaries for election workers.

LANGUAGE ACCESS FOR EVERY LANGUAGE AT EVERY VOTING LOCATION

*I*n the 2020 Primary Election, we were nervous about many new processes and services being implemented for the first time in an actual election. Among them, video conferencing for language assistance in the federally mandated languages at the time (Spanish, Vietnamese, Chinese, and Korean) was planned for and implemented successfully. I'm glad we could offer in-language assistance to voters and it enabled them to exercise their right to vote without the anxiety of not understanding their materials or ballots. During a debrief of the 2020 Primary Election, disability rights advocates made a helpful suggestion, stating that, though not required, OCROV could take further initiative to also offer assistance to voters who communicated through American Sign Language (ASL).

After much back and forth with the video conferencing service provider and our vendor for ASL interpreters, we were able to coordinate ASL assistance to all voting locations in time for the 2020 General Election. After figuring out the technical aspect of bringing ASL interpretation live at Vote Centers, we needed to ensure that the election workers at every voting location knew how to operate and assist voters when it came to this feature. This would become a joint effort between Outreach (language assistance), Election Services (support for voters with disabilities), IT (technology to assist voters), and Training (election worker training) to ensure all pieces from the different departments would be covered. Orange County's offering of ASL interpretation continues to be recognized as a leader in providing service to voters with disabilities and has since been replicated by other election offices.

For languages beyond the federally mandated languages and ASL, OCROV contracted with a third party provider that provided interpreter support for 200+ languages. Although the interpreter would not have subject matter expertise in voting or elections, the interpreter could work with OCROV staff and CSRs to effectively provide service and support to voters needing language assistance. This year-round service was available during years with election cycles and years without election cycles as well to ensure language access for every language at every voting location and beyond.

OCTOBER 2020

PARTNERSHIPS BETWEEN
THE ELECTION OFFICE AND MEDIA

With Election Day nearing and operations ramping up, media interest in our work grew exponentially. What were days or even weeks with just a handful of media inquiries turned into an overflow of emails and phone calls asking for interviews, tours, and general information. What questions and topics the media reached out about could reliably inform our office about the public sentiment and what was on their mind.

Although feeling nervous about interacting with the media, I took the approach that the media was doing their job in reporting news that the public wanted to learn more about and I was similarly doing my job in helping to get the word out about what our office did. Over the course of four years, I was able to build good relationships with journalists, reporters, and producers, and our office was rewarded with being sought out to provide an election official's perspective and accurate and timely information. Also, the media would seek us out first if someone had reported a tip related to voting and the election, and we would have the opportunity to address it before it made it to the news. If it were proven to be bogus, the media would often choose not to even publish it at all, rather than exploit it for clicks and cause more confusion and anxiety for the American public.

I remember one reporter who worked independently without a film crew and took all footage on his cell phone. Initially, we were a bit flustered by the amount of requests he made of us during our busy time, but we wanted to be accommodating, especially if it would lead to more understanding by the public and greater trust. Eventually, it did pay off; we had a chance to see the finished product, and his footage was comparable to the footage we had seen filmed by national mainstream media. The reporter's producers were happy with the result and gave the reporter a promotion for reporting on voting and the election.

One specific scene I recall the reporter filming was the printing of the ballots in our Printing and Graphics division. The reporter shared a line from the producers that evoked a sense of pride in the work we had done: "It must have smelled like democracy." In reality, it likely smelled un-theatrically strongly of paper and ink, but the sentiment was sweet and much appreciated, especially as elections offices were used to addressing claims that doubted our abilities and integrity.

Building strong and positive relationships with the media during the downtime and even at the cost of resources and attention during busy periods paid off dividends when it came to difficult and tense situations. We built a reputation of being accessible, responsive, and supportive with the media, which led to media outlets recommending our office to talk to when it came to voting and elections. Thus, our repeated presence in the media naturally highlighted our office as a leader in voting and elections locally, statewide, and nationally.

Though we had received interest from international media in the past, the 2020 General Election received more international media than I had ever seen before. We had reporters from Norway, Japan, and France who wanted to look at our office and film b-roll footage. They often had a separate interview with Neal prior to the tour, and I would escort them around the premises. We dealt with a wide range of media, from high school and college students reporting for their school's newspaper to Reuters, whose articles would be picked up widely by the PR Newswire. It was common to find stories about OCROV and photos and videos of our office by smaller media news outlets throughout the country and even the world.

The media had favorites of what they liked to film, such as the vote-by-mail ballots being processed, whether that would be being manually organized by rows and rows of election workers or the vote-by-mail ballots being scanned and sorted by machines when they arrived back in the office. There was also a favorite shot I liked to show in the mezzanine of the warehouse, where the media could have a bird's-eye view of the entire warehouse. Once a reporter posted videos or shots that their producers liked, other reporters would get word and come out to our office to get their own shots.

Since the media has the power to affect public opinion and trust, interacting with the media was heavily controlled in our office. Neal was the official spokesperson, and I supported with media tours, background information, and interviews as assigned. Neal and I developed a strong working relationship on handling the media, which was helpful while fulfilling the many media inquiries that came in as the election period became busier. I was fortunate to have opportunities to speak on NPR, national television, and panels with some of the country's most distinguished voting and election experts.

To counter the narrative that voting by mail was unsafe and unsecure, Neal decided to host a major press conference in partnership with then-Secretary of State Alex Padilla (the state's chief election official at the time) and Orange County District Attorney Todd Spitzer. In the press conference, District Attorney Spitzer was invited to give remarks on the County's response plan and criminal ramifications for people who attempted to participate in fraudulent activities. Preparation for the press conference was a big lift for our warehouse team as well. Neal had a strong desire to display all our vote-by-mail ballots in one photo, which put a lot of pressure on the team to print and organize nearly 2 million ballots to be shipped immediately after the press conference and on the same day.

On the morning of October 5, I was bustling to organize the massive line of photographers and media reporters occupying the entire backlot of our office. The lack of newsworthy activities due to nearly everyone staying indoors to avoid COVID-19, the controversy around voting by mail, and Neal's strong relationships with the media resulted in a very impressive turnout by the media. The number of attendees was probably only comparable to the media preview at the Honda Center just three weeks prior. For such large-scale events, it wasn't uncommon for me to play a role akin to Neal's executive assistant, keeping a line of people who wanted to speak to him or do an interview, while also taking photos for our own social media accounts.

Against the backdrop of semi-trucks loaded with all of Orange County's official vote-by-mail ballots, Secretary Padilla joined

District Attorney Spitzer and Neal to discuss voting options and the County's comprehensive plan to safeguard the election while providing residents access to observe the voting and ballot processing procedures. The purpose of this press conference was to inspire more confidence in the security of voting by mail and I would say that this played a role in the high percentage of voters choosing to vote by mail. When we looked at the results, we saw the highest turnout for voters choosing to vote-by-mail in the 2020 Presidential General Election (nearly nine in ten voters voted).

FAKE BALLOT BOXES ARE NOT FAKE NEWS (UNFORTUNATELY)

As we drew closer to the election, we faced a relentless onslaught of new challenges. Shortly after vote-by-mail ballots were delivered to voters in Orange County, a viral social media post drew heated discussion on the process for returning completed ballots. In a photo, a partisan field operative posed in front of a dark cabinet illegally labeled as an "Official Ballot Drop Off Box" and captioned it with his support for a candidate and asked others to directly message him for convenient drop-off locations.

The post was quickly picked up by the media and many other political campaign operatives. The situation continued to escalate as a statewide partisan organization started fighting back online to defend themselves and the legitimacy of their ballot drop boxes. Eventually, the Secretary of State's office and Attorney General's office got involved and began monitoring and investigating the situation.

It was a Sunday when this incident blew up. I was talking to a fellow manager in her office when I was called to address something else and I accidentally left my phone behind on her desk.

When I returned to pick up my phone, she told me that she had never seen a phone buzz so much. As the Community Outreach manager, I had all of our social media accounts linked to my phone and email so my phone would buzz any time we would receive an engagement (like a retweet or mention) online. For this event, our messaging was along the lines of "our office is aware of a fake ballot drop box and we are working with the Secretary of State's office and proper authorities for any further action." What we said publicly was very boilerplate and non-divisive, but internally we knew this situation was anything but normal.

Sometime later, I remember walking into the warehouse and saw Neal with the Warehouse manager, who was pushing a dolly with the fake ballot drop box from in the photo. The moment I saw the cabinet, whatever was on my mind to ask Neal didn't matter anymore. Seeing the cabinet made me feel like it should be in the custody of law enforcement and put in the evidence room.

They put the cabinet in the Tally Room, where you could see it from the outside. And as I was looking at it, I was just thinking how this was not a normal election. Instead, it was one where people were willing to break rules, cheat, and lie to win, and we as election officials were in the middle of it.

When it was all said and done, we had received over 1,000 new messages/tweets/mentions, which was wild considering every notification pinged my phone! Due to this incident, the field operative who appeared in the picture was publicly disgraced and the statewide partisan organization disassociated themselves from him. He no longer had a community to support him. In retaliation, he wanted someone to blame and blamed our office. He made some thinly veiled remarks and threats that caused OCROV to work with SWAT teams to do a sweep of our office. The team was alerted of his hostile behavior, and our environment was checked for potential "booby traps" or anything that we should be careful about. Neal kept us updated on any developments and we felt momentarily relieved but didn't want to let our guard down. It's better to be prepared than not.

ACTIVE SHOOTER WORRIES AND WILDFIRE RISKS

Neal advised us to be careful of the potential risk of an active shooter, which made it very scary at the time and even now. Our office had never done any active shooter training or had plans for it. And I couldn't help but think how exposed our front office was, which really made me sad because they would be the first ones affected. My concerns continued to grow as I thought of situations in which the perpetrators made it to the back office where the rest of our team operated from. I completed active shooter training in the past when I worked in the California State Senate as a District representative as my first job out of college.

After hearing about these potential risks, I began thinking how something that was theoretical had suddenly become a very real and potential possibility. When I went home, I talked to Howie about it. And it's sad, but we made plans on what I would do if there was an active shooter. Like where I would run outside to the employee entrance and how Howie would pick me up from a secluded corner. If I had to stay in the office, the location that I picked for me to hide in was next to my refrigerator behind my desk where there was a little space to fit into, if it were to happen.

It was very scary and I lost a lot of sleep over this. As we started counting down to the election, I always thought like "Is it going to be today?" and was glad at the end of each day that it wasn't today, but I continued to wonder if it would be tomorrow…. It was that way every day leading up to Election Day. I distinctly remember on election day thinking, If it's going to be any day, it's going to be today.

Unprecedented challenges began heating up as the election approached, quite literally. The madness that came when the wildfires happened definitely affected voting. We were scheduled for pop-up voting on the same day that the fires had gotten really bad overnight because of the winds. With the fires raging, we had to find safe ways of providing voting opportunities while keeping both people and ballots safe.

It was scary because we were receiving evacuation orders. It was tense because we were in full election mode, but members of my team had to go home during the day to pack up their belongings. They simultaneously had to deal with the election and the fires, and the potential threat that their home might not be there at the end of the day.

My neighborhood was not in the evacuation zones, but we were adjacent to the areas that were. The morning of one of our events, we were scheduled to hold a pop-up voting event in Peters Canyon, which was right by the hills on fire, and when we looked outside in the parking lot, we saw the sky ablaze. I arrived around 4:30 a.m. and talked to the staff, and they mentioned how they didn't want to go out and expressed their concern about the poor air quality.

We were very worried because the air quality was so bad; it was gray, black, and the sky was orange. There were ashes on our cars, and since pop-up voting was all outdoors it was impossible to avoid. Staff members were very scared, so I had to make a decision at that time. I called Neal around 5:00 a.m. and said the staff did not feel comfortable going out and I did not feel comfortable sending them because of these fires. If the fire really did get bad and it got to our pop-up voting location, it would take around two hours to break down.

I made my case to Neal and Neal understood that there was a problem, but also he had to balance at the same time that we had published this in our voter information guide, telling people to go vote there. We also had coordinated this with the facility we were using, and they also messaged it out to their own community members. But in the end, Neal had enough information from the emergency operation command center (EOC) who were messaging, "Do not drive into this area right now because this is a potential high fire zone." I think Neal felt we had enough signals to say we could close operations because we didn't want to be in a situation where we could've done more to save ballots or protect our people.

To inform the public, I worked with staff on a social media post to get the word out that pop-up voting was canceled for the day. I sent the pop-up voting team to support internal needs (for example, in the warehouse or the front office), but there was no way we could send them out in good conscience if things got bad. In the end human life comes first, but it would also mean the loss of equipment like the mobile voting unit that costs over $50,000, priceless ballots that had been already filled out that we might not be able to rescue in time, and the voting equipment itself. The trucks, the people, and everything else would be at risk.

We had to make a tough call, but in response to that we decided to hold two additional emergency pop-up voting events. In a week's time we found space in Anaheim Hills and Ladera Ranch to provide additional opportunities for voters to vote. There went our plans to have some rest and breaks in between our events. I think it was the right thing to do for the voters because we did make it so that it provided voting opportunities closer to the areas that were impacted by the wildfires.

During the fires, our office had to coordinate with the sheriff's office to collect the ballots that were in the fire evacuation zones. We also had to publicize on social media the ballot drop boxes and Vote Centers that would be closed due to the fires. That was very scary to have a police escort to an area where there was a pronounced risk of wildfires spreading to. There were coned-off areas; the sheriffs were not allowing people to go back to their homes on the other side. But they provided extra-special access to our ballot drop box team and Election Services team to go to the boxes and Vote Centers to receive ballots and our equipment and bring them back to the office. All while praying that nothing would get consumed in the fires when this would come to pass. Luckily, no ballots or people were damaged during this time, and nothing drastic affected the boxes themselves.

Additionally, the emergency evacuation centers worked with our office to provide information to individuals and families who wanted to vote and did not grab their ballot on their way out of their homes. Our approach was if you need something, just let us know and we will work to make sure you have access to voting. Even in a fire, you still have the right to cast a ballot. Democracy is still in action, and it doesn't stop for fires.

Honestly, that was really the sentiment of this election. Even in a global pandemic, even with fires raging, we did not move the election date. Election officials remain dedicated to making sure it continues. We have so many election workers and administrators who are willing to answer the call and protect democracy at any cost. And what an honor it was for me to be a part of that.

We got a lot of media calls during the fires. They were asking us, "What are you going to do?" "How is this affecting people?" Really, the media was just hungry for any information they could get on the election. At one point, they wanted to interview a member of the ballot collection team, but Neal took the interview and talked about how he worked with the sheriff's office. And it was beneficial that Neal had connections within the county who were willing to help us.

I think the media was a good partner to get the word out about the Vote Centers or ballot drop boxes being closed. It was helpful to have them spread accurate information, they could easily have chosen to not report on it or even put us in a bad light. But instead they talked about it very objectively and were rather supportive, the sentiment being: How else can you vote if your options are closed?

I really think about how having the support of the media is necessary for a successful operation. And you don't get support from the media as a transaction because it's something that is built over time. Trust is built and you really develop that relationship, and that's something that was unique about our office. Not just before or after the pandemic, but during it, how we were so accessible to the media. Although the constant presence of media can be draining, I think it paid off.

Media helping amplify our messaging and updates was helpful during this time. Without their help, it could have been more tiring for our office to reach our audience. It was also a good example of how an election administrator can work with media. As advice to other counties, I would recommend they find their "media champions" and let them understand what it takes to run an election and understand that media are the ones to relay the information to the public. Rather than being afraid, take interest and learn who they are, and have them learn who you are. Then, you will have a shared goal of educating the public.

A FAKE VOTE CENTER IS NOT
FAKE NEWS (UNFORTUNATELY)

As with every election, it was nothing new to be consistently informed of Republican activities by Democrats, or what the Democrats were doing by Republicans. But in the entire time I'd worked with OCROV, I had never dealt with reports of a fake voting location.

This was a first for me. All I could think was "How are they trying to fake a Vote Center?" I couldn't believe it. It was possible that I was a bit biased and blinded because I knew what our branding looked like, and I would clearly recognize a replica. But to the average voter, I realized they might not know. And what made it even worse about this specific fake Vote Center was that it was targeted toward Vietnamese immigrant communities, where some individuals did not have a strong grasp of English.

This hit home for me. Their targets could have easily been my parents and other immigrants, who often put their faith and trust into their community members who speak the same language as they do to navigate government programs and assist with legal needs. Unfortunately, there are some people in every community who use this familiarity for their own benefit.

Like many children of immigrants, I often helped my parents fill out paperwork and served as an interpreter at meetings and medical appointments. Unfortunately, I never learned Vietnamese and I was grateful for having bilingual staff at OCROV who could help serve as a bridge between OCROV staff and our language communities.

The office's Vietnamese community liaisons pointed out to me that some local Vietnamese advertisements were displaying this location as if it were a real Vote Center. They had a tent there, not one branded like ours, but it was hard to prove to voters who didn't know what to look for or were only reading what was in a more familiar language for them.

I remember Neal was up in a meeting when this blew up and I was pacing back and forth outside his door. I was trying to make eye contact with him through his blinds and trying to telepathically tell him I had something important I needed to tell him. I'm sure that was unusual for Neal to see because I didn't usually like to pace in front of his door. (Normally I would have asked the staff who sat nearby to call me when his door was open and Neal was available.) But I decided that this was too important of an issue so I would just stand outside until he was ready.

Eventually I got through to Neal, and he couldn't believe it either. I just shared the reports that I had received from the field, and then talked to the Election Services manager about sending one of the Vote Center supervisors to visit and see what was going on.

And then we heard back from the supervisor, who confirmed what we were hearing. Unfortunately, the supervisor did not speak Vietnamese so he couldn't read the several signs that appeared to be voting-related. While to us it looked odd, to the average person it could look authentic.

I saw a video of this site on Twitter and shared it with Neal. In the video, activists went to the back of this "Vote Center" and engaged with people who were wearing political campaign shirts and carrying a box of ripped-up vote-by-mail envelopes. The activists began accusing the supposed volunteers at this fake voting site of corrupting the election. I was shocked and shared the video with Neal.

The unofficial "Vote Here" signs scribbled on by a marker were evidence of misrepresenting a voting location.

In the end, it was a lot of "he said, she said" regarding what they claimed they were doing, but I feel like the video was indisputable evidence. In fact, candidates went on TV shows and gave a phone number for a voting hotline that was connected to this fake voting location. You would think it would go to our office, the official and nonpartisan election office, but the person calling it would not be reaching us. It was really frustrating to have to combat the fake news being spread, especially concerning where to vote and how to receive assistance.

COMMAND CENTER OPERATIONS

About two weeks before Vote Centers opened, we converted one of our large conference rooms into a Command Center. The screen we normally used for meetings and presentations now displayed average wait times at Vote Centers and the number of ballots issued to in-person voters. The layout of the Command Center was slightly adjusted every election, but the teams assigned to the Command Center were constant. The Command Center staff was a combination of members from four main teams: 1) Operations, 2) Election Services, 3) Training, and 4) IT Services. Before Vote Centers opened, the Operations team began managing the radio system that monitored the status of vote-by-mail ballot collections from the official ballot drop box sites. When Vote Centers were about to open, these operations were moved into the Command Center to centralize all our election operations.

The Election Services team members were the experts when it came to voting location and facility logistics. Recruitment of voting locations began months in advance of the election. With the transition from polling places to Vote Centers, several more specific considerations and requirements were used to determine voting locations. During the process of evaluating and securing Vote Centers, the Election Services team would build relations with the facility contacts. They would take note of any special considerations unique to each facility and relay this message to the election workers assigned to that location for the voting period. The Election Services team also designed the floor plans for how the voting equipment would be arranged to ensure optimal flow, and accessibility was available at every voting location. In the Command Center, this team was primarily responsible for addressing any facility-related issues.

The Training team members were the subject matter experts of Vote Center operations. Every hired election worker, or Vote Center CSR, needed to complete three days of training before they were assigned to work at a Vote Center. They were taught everything from opening and closing the polls, to issuing ballots to in-person voters, to documenting the chain of custody for voting equipment and ballots. Prior to the training period, this team worked closely with Operations to ensure that various scenarios, from most common to least expected, were considered and prepared for. The Training team provided the Command Center with the knowledge of how to resolve specific situations that might occur when processing voters at the Vote Center.

The IT team worked to resolve any tech issues that might occur within the Command Center or at the Vote Center. All Vote Centers communicated with the Command Center with a variety of technical equipment, and staff needed to periodically confirm that everything was running smoothly. For seamless operations, the IT team was constantly checking the active status and signal strength from each voting location. If any issues would arise, the IT team would proactively contact the Vote Center and begin troubleshooting immediately.

Aside from the team working in the Command Center itself, there were also teams referred to as Rapid Deployment Teams (RDT) on the field across the county. RDTs were ready to respond to various requests and could reach sites quickly. They were skilled in troubleshooting equipment issues and would occasionally replace equipment if the issue could not be resolved immediately onsite.

Our last team was our Vote Center supervisors. Each supervisor oversaw four to six Vote Centers within a small area of the county. They were tasked with visiting each Vote Center at least twice throughout the day to check in on general operations and assist if/where needed. Supervisors completed additional training to prepare them for more unique and urgent situations that CSRs might not be able to resolve on their own.

Before the voting period began, managers from the four teams selected a few of their team members to be assigned to the Command Center until the end of the election. The Command Center had two leads and reported to the Operations manager. The co-leads facilitated a training session for the new Command Center members as the various teams would come to work together and bring their own strengths for the final two weeks of the election.

When Command Center training began, the room was typically filled with mixed emotions. At this point, most of those assigned to the Command Center had spent months and countless hours preparing for the election, and it felt surreal to know that Vote Center doors would be opening and begin servicing voters. On the other hand, the Command Center was a completely new assignment, with new expectations and protocols to follow for proper escalation and resolution. While the members may have been with the Registrar of Voters for a while, this would be many of their firsts working with members of other teams as a new team.

The Command Center operated similarly to a call center. A phone number was shared with the various teams on the field as a primary contact to reach the Registrar of Voters office. When a call was received, a staff member in the Command Center recorded the issue in an online ticketing system and either resolved the call immediately or escalated the ticket appropriately. Questions could be as small as a request for more pens or as large as a regional power outage. Tickets were classified into three categories (minor, major, or critical) and were addressed as soon as possible.

The first day of Command Center operations focused on the set-up of the voting room. All voting equipment and supplies were packed by the warehouse team and delivered to the voting location a few days before the voting period. Upon arrival, the CSRs were to locate the equipment, confirm everything had been received, and begin setting up the room as outlined in the layout plans. At this stage, most of the calls received in the Command Center revolved around how to properly power test all equipment and secure the facility for the first day of voting.

Staff arrived early on the first day of voting, October 24. The Command Center was ready by 7 a.m., with many of the members arriving as early as 6 a.m. Though it was only the first day, we had already received some voicemails from some CSRs who were feeling sick or running late. Any calls related to illness, COVID-19 or not, were immediately forwarded to our HR department and were not ticketed in our online system. In the event a Vote Center would be short staffed due to an absence, an available employee would be assigned or reassigned to fill the gap in the meantime.

The number of calls started to pick up rapidly as the morning progressed. Despite the volume of calls, it was rare to receive a call with a major or critical issue. Oftentimes, it was a minor question or request, and most CSRs were calling for additional confirmation and clarity. For the first few hours or days, the calls were more to provide reassurance to the CSRs or to remind them of what was covered in their training program. Even in their nervousness, it was reassuring to see CSRs call the Command Center because they cared about the election and wanted to ensure everything was being done properly and without error.

Over the course of the voting period, we had received and responded to thousands of calls across all our Vote Centers. Following the end of the election, we filtered through each and every ticket to find common issues that we could improve election worker training on. We also reported the most critical issues to the Secretary of State's office, as requested after every election.

POP-UP VOTING BEGINS

In 2018, OCROV debuted a mobile voting unit to bring full-service voting opportunities to underrepresented populations and high-density locations. The pop-up mobile voting unit was the first of its kind in California and drew inspiration from pop-up stores and restaurants that often attracted positive public attention in areas with high traffic. The mobile unit had a custom wrap to match the marketing and branding plan OCROV had undertaken across the entire agency. The pop-up mobile voting unit was utilized throughout the 2020 election cycle, and in the March Presidential Primary election, the team embarked on an ambitious eleven-day tour across the county.

We were really excited to be able to plan pop-up events to not be back to back, as they had been in the previous election, so that the team could get breaks in between and not get exhausted. We had at least one pop-up site in each supervisorial district, in both public spaces and smaller community-based locations.

We had a great pop-up voting team and trainers from the Training team who understood the Vote Center operations and knew what they were doing. Despite having a great team, it was a huge shock when we went to our first event and came face to face with the huge amount of distrust and misinformation around vote-by-mail voting. There was a lot of skepticism around voting by mail and a huge push to vote in-person overall.

A pop-up voting team member who had done pop-up voting before was very comfortable and familiar with pop-up voting. This individual knew that in-person voting often came with small, short bursts of busy periods followed by periods of downtime. We were in South Orange County for a pop-up event and he had planned to go on nice walks during his breaks, and go rest by the water during lunch. But little did we know that the day would not be what we'd expected.

I went to our first day of pop-up voting to make sure that everything would go smoothly, but as we were setting up, a line had already started forming. That had never, ever happened before for any type of pop-up voting during my entire time supporting OCROV.

By the time we were finished setting up, the line was about forty to fifty people long. From the table, the line extended from the pavement at the grass all the way out and far beyond the space we had marked for line management. Furthermore, we could not even start processing voters yet because we had to wait until 8 a.m. The line was beginning to form at 6:30 a.m. and just continued to grow.

Fortunately, the IT manager and the Operations manager both lived in South Orange County and visited to support our team. They were shocked at the turnout, and the line continued to grow until toward the end of the day (3 p.m.). Since we were not processing voters as fast as new voters were joining, the line never really died down. The IT manager and Operations manager ended up requesting more voting booths to accommodate the number of voters.

We had a grand plan, a great display of our voting booths under our large, branded canopy (roughly thirty feet by ten feet), but with the ongoing pandemic we had to space out the voting booths at least six feet apart and they could not fit nicely underneath. It definitely became more challenging with the number of voters to make sure everything was going smoothly. Luckily, we had more support from staff who were able to come and stay all day.

This also became our first opportunity to put our new CSR training to test. For example, we had a disinfecting procedure after every voter in a voting booth, and we were able to see how feasible it would be. I distinctly remember also calling our Vote Center Help Desk line to put in a request for more cleaning products because we were going through our wipes much faster than we'd anticipated. After our first pop-up event, we decided that it would be best to have enough supplies on hand for two events so that we didn't run out of materials.

I remember people being very feisty or angry at check-in. Many people were not wearing masks or were wearing things that were inflammatory. We had to de-escalate numerous situations and do our best to create a safe and nonpartisan voting environment.

There were also poll watchers. They kept their space, but they set up their lawn chairs and watched us for half the day. They were courteous, and when they left they told us that we were doing a good job. Yet it was still tiring, knowing that they were watching us all day and were motivated by the goal of finding something wrong. They didn't trust us and they wanted us to know that.

At the end of the first pop-up voting day, we found we had served more than 1,300 voters according to our ePollbook check-ins. Our team who serviced these voters was only about ten people large, many of them permanent staff who normally would not be there. It felt like a busy election day rather than the first in-person voting day. Thinking back, I don't think anyone took a break. We had tried, even creating a schedule for breaks and meals, but we were more focused on serving voters who were anxious and worried, and helping them as quickly as possible. I believe that is a testament to the wonderful work that election workers are doing but a dire call for additional resources for election officials as well. These people were willing to sacrifice themselves to have people trust and have faith in the democratic process.

So many sacrifices were made and so many more continue to be made to fight the distrust and commit to the under-recognized work. It often goes underappreciated. It truly made me appreciate my team, but it was also sad that even just a lunch break was too much to ask for at times. A sense of guilt would settle in if a CSR needed to step away for a break or lunch.

When I reported back how pop-up voting went at the management and OPS meeting, a manager asked if it would be like this every single day of pop-up voting. What I had witnessed at our first pop-up voting event for this election was a preview of what massive in-person voting turnout could be like for our team. This was just one day at one voting location. Is this what it would be like at 168 Vote Centers during the regular in-person voting period? Did we have the capacity to handle that?

We knew we'd somehow make it work. Failure was never an option.

NOVEMBER 2020

THE DAY BEFORE ELECTION DAY

When it started to get late in the office the night before Election Day, coworkers would urge each other to make sure they had eaten, drunk water, and recently stood up from their desk. These were small acts of kindness to show we cared about each other's well-being, even if we all knew that the election was the top priority.

As coworkers began to call it a night and head home, we also urged others to head home and would walk each other to their cars. With time running out, there was little we could do to effect real change when we were counting down hours to the polls opening. At this point, we knew we needed to get enough rest to make it through Election Day and whatever it could bring. All checklists had been checked multiple times, and walkthroughs throughout the office and warehouse had been completed to ensure we were as prepared as we could be for whatever waited for us the next day. By now, we accepted we'd done what we could humanly do and reminded ourselves that we'd gone through difficult elections before and could do it again.

Once you got home, maybe your household was still awake or maybe they weren't and you were greeted by a dark home. If you were lucky, you would have a few precious moments to hear about your partner's day and could help out with a few chores as you felt guilty for your lack of presence at home over the past few months. Maybe they had food waiting for you or maybe you had to pick up late-night food for dinner. Our office was across the street from a twenty-four-hour McDonald's, which was a blessing and a curse. At least there was always McDonald's, we'd say.

After showering and preparing for bed, I'd lie in bed only half-heartedly trying to sleep. What I actually did was run through all of the things I had done during the day, trying to see if I had missed anything or would need to do something once I got into the office. I'd send countless emails to myself with only the subject line as a reminder to my future self. I didn't want to forget anything and didn't trust myself to remember it all without writing it down. The next morning, I'd wonder what message I was trying to leave for myself at 3 a.m.

I set multiple alarms to wake up and had an irrational fear of missing every single alarm, even though I would intermittently wake up and rise before the first alarm went off due to high levels of anxiety. No one else was awake at home by the time physical exhaustion took over. I was grateful for these small moments of peace and quiet as a stark contrast to the types of notifications I dealt with during the day:

- ★ My desk phone

- ★ My work cell phone for calls and emails

- ★ My personal cell phone

- ★ The office's intercom system

- ★ Radio communications. I carried a personal radio for the two weeks leading up to Election Day.

- ⋆ Unprompted media and VIP visits to the office

- ⋆ Social media comments on Facebook, Instagram, and Twitter in English, Spanish, and Vietnamese

- ⋆ My desktop for emails

- ⋆ Escalated calls from the phone bank

For the ones who support you and make it possible to be an election official, Election Day and the day before is just another day. Sure, they might go to vote at a voting location or drop off their ballot, but their day will be nothing like yours. And you are grateful for that. You hope that they never have to make the sacrifices you have and endure the challenges you've gone through.

E-0: ELECTION DAY

No two Election Days are the same, but they usually follow the same beginning. You wake up at a ridiculously early hour, probably around 3 a.m. or 4 a.m., and mentally prepare yourself for the day ahead by running through possible scenarios. There is no shortage of them. I would arrive at the office around 5 a.m. to prepare the Media Room and work through the reminder emails I sent myself. The Media Room dealt with VIPs, election observers, and media.

If I had extra time, I'd buy breakfast pastries for my team the night before and bring them as a small gesture of support on what would be a tough day ahead. I tried to be thoughtful and show my appreciation where I could, but it provided little solace, considering what they could be dealing with on Election Day.

Yet, despite the usual similar beginnings, the morning of Election Day, November 3, 2020 will forever stand out in my mind.

A QUIET REFLECTION AND ACCEPTANCE

It was the morning of Election Day, and I arrived early at the office, seeking a moment of quiet before the day would unfold. The dimly lit office was still, and the hum of servers and the soft blue glow from computers in the darkness provided an odd sense of solitude. While other office workers were allowed to work at home, my personal office, a modest space, had become my home for the last eight months.

In those quiet moments, I couldn't help but reflect on the intersectionality of my identities as an Asian American woman working as an election official, particularly in Orange County. I thought of my parents and their beginnings. They had arrived in the U.S. as Vietnamese refugees who couldn't speak English and sacrificed their own personal hopes and dreams so that I could pursue mine.

I wondered if they were proud of me and if my sacrifices would repay them for all they'd done for me. They had an idea of what my work was, something related to voting and elections, but I lacked the ability to speak with them fluently about what I did in detail. Describing election administration in English is already complex enough. Adding in language barriers and a significant generational and cultural gap made it even more difficult.

The weight of responsibility rested heavily on my shoulders; the voters of Orange County were depending on me and the OCROV team to ensure that the election ran smoothly. The challenges over the past year had been immense, from dealing with the hardships of the COVID-19 pandemic to threats of violence. As an Asian American, I had also faced the added burden of hearing derogatory terms associating the virus with my heritage.

On the news and repeated by prominent leaders, COVID-19 was often described as the China flu, China plague, China virus, Wuhan virus, and kung flu. This carelessness led to Asian Americans of all ages and backgrounds being targeted for discrimination and violent attacks. More than 11,000 acts of hate against Asian Americans and Pacific Islanders have been reported to Stop AAPI Hate, a national coalition fighting against racism and racial injustice targeting Asian Americans and Pacific Islanders, and untold more unreported acts have occurred since March 2020 and the start of the pandemic.

As I reflected that morning, I wondered, *Is putting my life on the line to save democracy enough to be considered American, despite being of Asian descent?*

It was clear that Asian Americans were often seen as perpetual foreigners, a racist and xenophobic stereotype in which naturalized and even native-born citizens are perceived by some members of society as foreign because they belong to a minority ethnic or racial group.

Most days, I rarely had the space or time to ponder. If anything were to happen, it would happen today. At this moment, all I could do was wonder:

★ Is there anything I can do now to prepare for challenges that will come later today?

★ Is there anything I can do to protect my team?

★ Do Howie, my parents, and my family know how much I love them?

★ Will I make it to another day after Election Day?

★ Did I make sure everything was taken care of at home before I left, in case this morning is the last time I will leave home?

★ If I were to die today, what can I do now to make it easier for my loved ones and team members?

My heart began to race from strong feelings of fear, thinking of anything and everything that could get in the way. I had already survived concerns of an active shooter, bomb threats, wildfires, a fake Vote Center, fake ballot drop boxes, and multiple protests.

What else could be next?

I contemplated my future at my desk alone in an empty office. I realized it wasn't worth trying to predict a future I couldn't see, and I accepted that I would willingly give all of me to play a role in saving democracy.

ELECTION MORNING BEGINS

Without fail, Neal would invite all of the managers to meet early on the morning of Election Day in a small conference room. This provided an opportunity for leadership to work through any major issues and bring up any challenges that would impact multiple teams. There was always an emphasis on communication; even if it wasn't good news or if it was difficult news, we knew it was important to share with each other. If not, the problems had a way of showing up and becoming worse later.

Command Center operators would also receive pertinent updates as they oversaw the entire election operation in a separate room within the election office. A dashboard showing the GPS locations of ballot drop box collections, Rapid Deployment Team GPS locations, and a map of all voting locations and ballot drop boxes projected on a large screen taking up an entire wall's width and length helped Command Center operators identify, track, and resolve issues. The Command Center operators helped facilitate collaboration and communication between teams. Members of the Training team and Election Services team were the core Command Center operators due to their strong background in Vote Center operations and aptitude for solving complex problems. Undoubtedly, they were instrumental in resolving small and medium issues and escalating any major problems.

The most important part of any operation is always the people. For running voting locations, it's the trained election workers who help voters cast a ballot and troubleshoot issues. Yet, election workers are not invincible. They are susceptible to being sick, catching COVID-19, and calling out (as they should). They can have family emergencies and have to leave town immediately. They may no longer be able to serve due to other unforeseeable circumstances. As election officials, we have to plan for this possibility and still ensure we have enough election workers and enough bilingual workers to fill these staffing holes.

We typically set backup staffing goals based on previous elections, but the 2020 General Election was unprecedented. We couldn't reference election planning documents from the last election conducted during a pandemic, which would have been the Great Influenza of 1918. In Orange County, we called this trained group of flexible election workers who could help with any role the "A-Team." Truly, the A-Team has saved the day many, many times, and much gratitude is owed to the volunteers and temporary workers who stepped up to the call of duty for democracy.

The Election Services team would be on-call to help with voting locations, accessibility needs, and supporting Vote Center Supervisors. Their strong relationships with location hosts literally helped open doors and ensure voting access at convenient locations throughout the county. Election Services was also responsible for managing the A-Team and the Vote Center Supervisors to ensure that operations at in-person voting locations were going smoothly.

The A-Team arrived at the Warehouse early on Election Day

and waited to receive an assignment from the Command Center. Without fail, every election office receives last-minute notifications from election workers that they can no longer fulfill their role. Sometimes, they will cite illness or a family or medical emergency. Sometimes, it could be nerves, anxiety, and fear. Sometimes, all of the above.

Whatever the reason, election officials had to urgently figure out how to fill this staffing need with little time and resources. That's where the A-Team came in—trained, and ready to rock and roll.

As the clock got closer and closer to polls opening at 7 a.m., field staff began to leave the office and we began to hear from election workers at each voting location. Rapid Deployment Team members were assigned regions within the county, so they could readily respond to any voting locations experiencing technical issues or needing supply replenishment. Vote Center supervisors made their rounds to the handful of voting locations they were assigned to, similar to how a regional manager would be responsible for stores in a certain region. Over the radio, calls from Supervisors confirming their assigned voting locations were ready started to trickle in.

Phonebank operators received a briefing on the latest updates, what to watch out for, and reminders before the general assistance line was opened up for calls from the public. As the first line of defense, phonebank operators were generally able to help most voters with basic inquiries. The busiest day would be Election Day. A team of a few dozen phone operators would field tens of thousands of phone calls in numerous languages. The Phonebank supervisor would review the voicemail messages and forward them to the various teams within the office so they could be properly addressed.

The front office would be converted to a supercharged voting location, which had the advantage of being connected to the central election office and senior staff could be called upon to the counter with relative ease. The Candidate and Voter Services team would become Vote Center CSRs and help the thousands of voters who would come to the central election office. The Pop-Up Mobile Voting team would also move to support processing voters in the front office. Due to the heightened paranoia and distrust sowed by candidates who campaigned on the diminishing integrity of elections, a record number of voters traveled to vote at the central elections office and drop off their ballots.

Although it was busy in 2020, it was not as busy as previous election cycles. Before Orange County transitioned to using electronic pollbooks and allowed voters to cast a ballot at any voting location, voters who needed to register to vote after the voter registration deadline could only do so at the central election office. In 2018, I remember being amazed by the long line that extended outside of our office and reached the street. I also distinctly remember helicopters above our office to capture footage of the long, long lines of voters waiting to cast a ballot.

The Warehouse becomes abuzz with energy, people, and lots of moving pieces and equipment during Election Day. Not only are there lots of workers, but many visitors can be found in the Warehouse. The visitors include candidates, campaign staff, political party representatives, volunteers, advocates, and curious members of the public. Overseeing a warehouse for voting and elections is truly a skill that only some can manage and master. Imagine the challenge of storing, moving, and organizing millions and millions of pieces of anything, much less ballots and voting equipment—it certainly is not an easy endeavor.

On Election Day, you can most certainly expect election observers looking for any issue to call attention to and ask basic questions about the voting and election process. Election administration is intentionally complicated to preserve its integrity. There are multiple layers of security, restricted access, and fail-safe fallbacks incorporated to execute the most secure election possible. There is arduous pre-election testing and post-election auditing to ensure that the voting equipment and results reported are accurate. All voting equipment and ballots have detailed chain of custody processes that all election workers are taught to follow and election officials monitor and check to confirm processes are being followed.

Those who question voting and elections should consider volunteering or working as an election worker and have a chance to see the multiple layers of security and assurance in every process. When people are not knowledgeable, seeding distrust is easy and casting doubt on things you aren't familiar with because you don't have the background or experience is easier than genuinely trying to learn and understand.

The Voter Data Services team works diligently to enter data and verify signatures on the envelopes containing voted ballots. Each member of the team has access to the secure voter database that can pull up the profile of every registered voter in the County. When comparing the signature on the envelope to the database, the team member has access to all signatures a voter has provided on a voter registration form. If you had re-registered multiple times (change of address, change of name, etc.), your signature may have slightly changed over the years, and seeing these signatures is helpful to ascertain whether the envelope's signature is truly yours.

The Outreach team helped ensure voters who needed language assistance could receive the same services and information as voters not needing language assistance. I oversaw the Outreach team, which holds a special place in my heart as we worked closely on many levels. Members of the Outreach team would be responsible for handling calls relayed from other teams to serve as the interpreter, video conferencing from voters who used a tablet at voting locations and needed language assistance, receiving calls from language community partners who referred voters directly to them, and more. For federally mandated languages Orange County was required to support, OCROV had a full-time staff member who was fluent and served as the office's community liaison. This provided a high level of service to the community and helped other staff members in navigating cultural nuances and linguistic barriers.

Even though I am not fluent in another language, my team trusted me to lead and support them to do their work. When I saw older generations needing language assistance, it reminded me of my parents, who also needed language assistance to navigate government programs and services when they first immigrated. Those who took the extra time to help them made all the difference in feeling welcomed in a new country. For me, working as an election official was a way of giving back to the community by helping newer immigrants and their families vote and repaying what was given to my family.

You just hope that what you do is enough. In my case, I hoped that our team was ready for Election Day.

7 A.M.: THE POLLS ARE NOW OPEN

By the time 7:00 a.m. rolled around, election officials and workers in the field were rushing to ensure all preparations were set by the time polls opened. It seemed like every worker was on their phone; managers were walking from the warehouse to the front office to their desk; and the line of voters outside seemed to grow longer and longer with each minute.

Then, we heard a beaming voice over the office's intercom.

"The polls are now open."

From this point, everyone knows that it's a matter of counting down the clock until 8:00 p.m. when the polls officially close and no more voting is allowed. However, a lot can happen between 7:00 a.m. and 8:00 p.m. and *nothing* is off the table.

Honestly, the actual Election Day was a blur. I know things happened, but it's possible that I've blocked much of my memory due to traumatic events or I have just forgotten over the time that has passed since that fateful day. For election officials in counties that offer more than one day of in-person voting, we treat every day of in-person voting as Election Day. I'll share a few memorable stories of what happened during the in-person voting period in the 2020 General Election in Orange County.

YOU'RE IN OR URINE?

It was already hard to deal with long lines prior to the pandemic, and the health and safety requirements made it even more difficult. Long lines spilled out to the parking lot and street at popular Vote Centers, which made it more difficult to manage voters in line. Even though there may not have been that many voters in line, the six-foot distance between each voter made the line feel much longer than it actually was. Some buildings required temperature checks before allowing people in, and we quickly had to work with locations as state law does not allow for voters to be turned away at the polls due to their internal temperature.

In the fall of 2020, many public buildings were still closed to the public. This included their bathrooms as these organizations and agencies cut back on staffing, including their custodial staff. Despite being generally closed to the public, some of these buildings still served as Vote Centers. We had no idea that these locations would open to the public but keep their bathrooms closed.

Unfortunately, this resulted in a situation where an elderly voter needed to use the restroom but did not want to leave his place in line or drive to another location that had bathrooms that were open to the public. We tried getting ahold of the decision-maker and going through the bureaucratic process to allow the voter to use the onsite restroom but it could not be done in time.

When I heard about this happening, I had to clarify—"Did you mean "you're in" or "urine?"—and it was the latter. The voter was embarrassed and we felt disappointed in ourselves that we had overlooked this potential scenario. Fortunately, this was the only instance during this election cycle and it spurred action to confirm all other Vote Centers had bathrooms available to the public.

For all future elections, confirming the availability of restrooms is now part of our election planning checklist (even in a pandemic when buildings are closed to the public).

WESTMINSTER BOMB SCARE

I was alerted by the Command Center about a suspicious unattended package at the Vote Center located at the Westminster Library. The threat seemed real enough and we didn't want any of the election workers or library staff to be harmed in trying to figure out whether it was a real threat or not. Vote Center staff were directed to shut down operations out of an abundance of caution while we notified and waited for the SWAT team to arrive and conduct their safety checks.

When I received this call, I thought that this was finally it—what I had feared and dreaded for the last six months. A major act of violence targeting election officials was unheard of but hinted at by election deniers. The feeling in the air was that anything was possible, both good and bad; more bad, though. We had already gone through so much: COVID-19, George Floyd protests, anti-Asian attacks, large gatherings of vaccine deniers, global supply challenges, shutting down the 2020 Summer Olympics and other sporting events, wildfires across the world, and more. At times, I was scared to even utter "What else could happen?" because it seemed like it preceded another major incident.

When election workers stopped voting operations for the SWAT team to arrive and assess the situation, we had to turn away voters, unfortunately. We provided the address of nearby alternate voting locations, but some voters were peeved. However, we didn't want to cause false alarms or start a massive panic by telling people there was a potential bomb. Election workers did their due diligence by setting up barriers and preventing voters from getting closer to where the suspicious package was.

Some of these voters must have contacted the voter protection hotlines for the Republican Party and Democratic Party because I received calls from both parties.

I distinctly recall feeling overwhelmed and unsure about what to do in this situation. I had never been in another situation where there was a real possibility that a bomb might set off and hurt my team. Although I was not in physical danger as I was stationed at the central election office miles away, I worried about the election workers, the library staff, and members of the public wanting to cast a ballot or check out a book.

The party representatives were upset and wanted to know why OCROV was preventing voters from being able to cast a ballot. I was speaking to each party's lead attorney for Orange County and knew that both were ready to litigate or call a judge and request an injunction at any moment. I decided to tell them that we were investigating a report of a bomb at this voting location and pausing voting operations until we received verification it was safe.

I'll always remember the reaction of one of the party representatives I was speaking to. After I shared the reason why we were pausing operations, there was a sharp gasp that was followed by heavy silence from the other side of the phone.

"I'm so sorry. Wishing you and your team godspeed."

Now, the worries these party representatives and I had prior to being notified about the bomb went out the window. They understood that we had to ensure the safety of our staff and voters first. Though we had a protocol for handling incidents like this, dealing with a potential bomb is not something most of us deal with on a daily basis. Yet, we couldn't be immobilized by our shock. We needed to take action—every second that passed meant there was even less time for voters to cast a ballot.

The SWAT team came and cleared the area. It was an unattended empty bag that was left behind and no one came back to get it. Though it turned out not to be an actual threat, it was reassuring to have confirmation that it was safe.

Slowly, the Vote Center CSRs reentered the voting location and had a brief moment to recenter themselves. Then, voters returned to the voting location—most unaware that there was just a bomb threat at the same site.

ELECTION FASHION: AMERICAN FLAGS AND CAMPAIGN ATTIRE

According to California's Election Code § 319.5, "electioneering" means the visible display or audible dissemination of information that advocates for or against any candidate or measure on the ballot within the one-hundred-foot limit specified of a voting location or ballot drop box. For example, wearing any clothing (hats, shirts, signs, buttons, stickers) that includes a candidate's name, image, logo, and/or supports or opposes any candidate or ballot measure is prohibited and considered to be electioneering.

Every election cycle, there are a few enthusiastic campaign supporters who either don't know that this type of electioneering is prohibited or intentionally seek out to challenge this statute. Sometimes, the individual is apologetic and changes into different attire without incident. Usually, they'll put on a jacket to cover the offending shirt. Some other times, there are individuals who fight tooth and nail and cause a scene, whether to bring attention to themselves as supposed "defenders" of democracy or their candidate.

For the 2020 General Election, campaign supporters were fired up and some were looking for every opportunity to showcase themselves as having their rights infringed upon and being unfairly treated. Causing conflict with election workers enforcing electioneering policies was an effective venue to draw attention to themselves and disrupt the election process.

Though this happens numerous times and in every election jurisdiction and in every election, a particular instance comes to mind of the kinds of ridiculousness election officials deal with. One unsuspecting Vote Center and its CSRs would have a very challenging day.

An individual wearing an American flag as a cape and a shirt encouraging the support of a particular presidential candidate marched into a Vote Center, determined to make it known who he was supporting. Eager to build support, he also brought campaign flags, flyers, and more to hand out. This would've been fine if he were attending a rally or a partisan event, but he wasn't. He was going to a Vote Center where other voters would be present and electioneering was prohibited.

When he came to the entrance of the Vote Center location, it was clear he was not just there to vote. In fact, he exclaimed, "The election is rigged—don't trust whatever they say. Make sure you vote for [candidate name]!" to all who were present. He tried handing out the giveaways he had brought but was stopped by two CSRs who sprang into action.

Until this voter came in, the Vote Center CSRs were having an uneventful day. Earlier in the voting period, there are fewer voters who come to vote in person. Now, they had to deal with a problematic voter intent on making a scene.

Voter Center CSRs utilized the tactics they learned in CSR training to de-escalate the situation. They spoke to him about the Elections Code and its purpose. They emphasized that willfully defying the Elections Code to corrupt the integrity of the election has consequences and used behavioral practices to calm him down. We reminded him that he could wear his attire and give out partisan materials in many other places but not here. We expressed that we would do the same for any other candidate and campaign and that he would feel uncomfortable if a supporter of the opposing candidate did the same thing.

Though it took longer than expected, the individual eventually relented and agreed to flip his shirt inside out and wear it while voting. Even though he expressed he'd ruin OCROV, and claimed his rights were being violated, a compassionate and firm, calm discussion can go a long way.

I know that this is not always the case. As politics become more and more contentious, these types of conflict could lead to physical violence and election officials and workers must be supported and protected.

LEAVE YOUR GUNS AT HOME; DON'T TAKE THEM TO THE VOTE CENTER

Leading up to Election Day, the discourse around the election became more and more tense and inclined toward violence. There were online organizing efforts of all types. Most were to encourage voter turnout through coordinating carpooling, phone banking, and door knocking. There were some whispers of potential violence, and it was scary to think about any of them becoming a reality.

During an appearance on far-right conspiracy theorist Alex Jones' program, Oath Keepers militia leader Stewart Rhodes said members of his militia would be at polling locations on Election Day to "protect" Trump voters. This threat was transmitted to government emergency centers across the country, and appropriate actions were taken to identify potential threats early on and prepare for any fulfilled threats on Election Day.

As election officials, we wanted to notify our election workers without causing them to unnecessarily fear and stress about potential threats of violence. We waited until we were advised by law enforcement agencies on what steps to take. More often than not, the threats were baseless and dismissed. Yet, as a senior manager in the elections office, I felt that I had that burden of knowledge and had to keep it together and not show my concerns to my team. I wanted to protect them as much as I could and pretend things were as normal as can be. Hardly anything was normal anymore, especially when everything changed due to COVID-19.

Fortunately, there weren't any incidents where an individual brought a gun to a voting location in Orange County in the 2020 General Election. Though nothing happened, the damage was done. My mind was already prepared for the possibility of it happening, and that meant walking through potential scenarios multiple times and creating response plans for each scenario. We affirmed our preparedness in the event it might happen in the future and doubled down on our commitment to protecting the voting process.

"MEET AT THE ELECTION OFFICE
FOR THE RALLY"

gencies that monitored internet activity for potential threats to voting and elections alerted us of the possibility of a protest being organized to take place at our elections office. I was no stranger to protests as I had previously worked for other government offices that also had their fair share of protests. However, the tension in the air this time around was different.

During the summer of 2020, there were numerous protests across the United States inspired by the death of George Floyd, the Black Lives Matter (BLM) movement, anti-Asian hate, anti-mask demonstrations, and candidate rallies, among many others. These rallies and protests had seen tensions running high and, in some instances, resulted in vandalism and violence.

Orange County was no exception. In fact, Huntington Beach was the birthplace of the anti-mask resistance and held several rallies where Trump supporters and BLM supporters collided with counter-protesters. As Orange County was home to several battleground congressional districts, what happened in Orange County would routinely make it onto national news, and movements seeking more recognition knew it would be strategic to make a splash here.

The Orange County Sheriff's Department (OCSD) and several local police departments across the county took extra precautions on Election Day and throughout the week in case protests flared up. Our elections office received a security briefing and reminded staff on emergency protocols should a protest become violent or impede the voting process.

I started to hear from other staff about a group with protest signs and red baseball caps forming outside of our office. We alerted OCSD and they immediately sent a few sheriff's deputies to our office to keep a close eye on the protestors. Eventually, the group decided to start chanting and marching on the sidewalk with their protest signs. It was fairly peaceful, which was a relief as we prepared for potential conflict and confrontations. I still avoided going outside and ordered lunch to be delivered to the office for my team, so we could take a proactive approach to staying safe.

Although there were no significant voter disruption events, protests, or demonstrations on Election Day, OCSD was ready to activate an operations center to monitor civil unrest for public safety and traffic management. As tensions over voting and elections continue to grow, it is necessary for election offices to work closely with local, state, and federal law enforcement agencies to ensure the safety of voters, election workers, and ballots and mitigate any potential and actual threats.

SIGNS OF HOPE AND POSITIVITY

Though the news and public discourse mainly focused on the negatives around the election, there were definitely positives as well. The Orange County Employee Association (OCEA) drops off pizza to feed workers at the central elections office every election without fail. The small acts of gratitude from voters who show appreciation to election workers help get them through the day. Whether it is as simple as a smile or a "thank you," every bit counts.

Personally, I remember the joy and pride voters had when casting their ballot. I remember seeing doctors and nurses coming to vote at the pop-up voting mobile unit when we were stationed near a hospital. They came to cast their ballot while wearing their doctor's coats and nurse uniforms. Knowing how little free time they had while they needed all hands on deck to fight COVID-19 before a vaccine was developed, it was moving. As tired as they were, our healthcare heroes knew it was important to vote, and so they did.

We'd see parents come into Vote Centers with their children, who were curious about this room with lots of equipment and materials they'd never seen before. Many of these children, I imagine, would be excited and eager to be a voter in the future after this experience. Some voters, mostly seniors, with their pets and their friends would come by before continuing with their day. We'd see individuals stopping by to cast their ballot while on a run or a bike ride. Children and grandchildren helped their parents and grandparents with translation to cast a ballot. The happenings of a Vote Center are just a slice of their lives, but all are connected by having their voices heard in the election.

It was particularly joyful when a newly naturalized citizen came in to cast their first ballot. They knew what it was like not to have the right to vote, so now having that ability wasn't taken lightly. They beamed with pride and were curious and eager to cast their vote. It was a much welcomed contrast to the doom and gloom we had heard about on the news around voting and elections.

Working as an election official can feel like a thankless job, and then, there are times when you feel so appreciated and proud to do this work. We cherish those times, and those moments and memories carry us through the more difficult times.

8 P.M: THE POLLS ARE NOW CLOSED

Similar to the morning announcement, there is a much-awaited announcement in the evening at 8 p.m. sharp.

"The polls are now closed."

When election officials hear this, we know we're in the home stretch of finishing Election Day. By no means are we finished; in fact, we are just starting the final chapter of Election Day. Yet, many breathe a sigh of relief, knowing that most of the day's work is behind us and we just have a little more to get through before we can go home and rest. Before we can be reunited with our families and check in on our pets. Before we can have a moment to ourselves and rest.

Prior to the polls closing, certain parts of the office would temporarily close to the public in order to prepare for Election Night operations. We needed to get ready for the return of ballots, equipment, and other materials from the 168 Vote Centers. Additionally, Neal gathered all of the election workers in the office together in the Warehouse for a quick debrief and to have dinner together. This was a chance to hear updates that might affect Election Night operations, to learn whether we had any VIPs onsite, and to organize a plan for the barrage of media, candidates, and campaign representatives who would be watching election results at our office in real-time and around the country.

At 8:05 p.m., OCROV would post the first round of election results. These initial results consisted solely of the vote-by-mail ballots that had been verified prior to Election Day. These generally represented a significant portion of the ballots cast and could be a good indicator of how much of the vote share would go to a candidate or which side of a proposition was more likely to win.

The challenging thing is that some districts and propositions applied to more than one county. This meant you had to check the websites of multiple counties on Election Night to know how your candidate or side was doing. If one of the counties you were monitoring was delayed or not technologically sophisticated, election results for a multicounty contest would have to be pieced together or wait for the Secretary of State to post cumulated results on its website for state and federal contests.

California Election Code states that voting is allowed until 8 p.m. on Election Night. OCROV had a separate group of workers to assist with closing ballot drop boxes on Election Night. This group, primarily made of volunteers who are county employees, was called the Ballot Drop Box Strike Force Team. A member of the Ballot Drop Box Strike Force Team would join the end of the line to drop off a vote-by-mail ballot and tell any voter seeking to get in line after 8 p.m. that it was now too late to do so. Once it did turn 8 p.m., Ballot Drop Box Strike Force Team members would either lock the ballot drop box or be in line ready to lock after the last person who stood in line before 8 p.m. finished dropping off their ballot. For in-person voting locations, there is a similar process.

After the last voter has cast their ballot, election workers can lock the door and start taking the necessary steps to return ballots and put away equipment and materials. Chain of custody forms were required for every piece of equipment and sets of materials. Multiple individuals needed to sign off and affirm that everything was accounted for. Any deviance was grounds for investigation and potentially serious consequences. Each Vote Center had its own mini-storage box where it could hold equipment and materials, and OCROV contracted with truck delivery services to move these boxes to Vote Centers and back to OCROV.

COLLECTION CENTERS

Returning voted ballots from 168 Vote Centers across Orange County's 792 square miles on Election Night was a logistical challenge. Vote Center CSRs were needed to stay at their assigned Vote Center to help close things down, but these voted ballots needed to return to the central elections office and be secured. Collection centers were OCROV's solution and had proven to be helpful in previous elections.

Collection Centers were created as temporary regional convening locations to streamline deliveries to the central elections office. After accounting for all voted ballots, Vote Center CSRs would secure them in their car and drive to the nearest collection center. Several Vote Centers were assigned to each collection center and assigned drivers would make multiple trips to the central elections office and back to the collection center until all voted ballots were returned. Each driver would be followed by another Vote Center CSR in their car to ensure that the ballots would safely make it to the Collection Center from the Vote Center.

Once at the Collection Center, Collection Center staff would follow a checklist to track what was returned by each Vote Center and sign off on chain of custody forms. After this process, the Collection Center had its own set of drivers to deliver voted ballots back to the central elections office in Santa Ana. OCSD deputies accompanied drivers from Collection Centers to the central election offices and provided security at the OCROV office to ensure the smooth transfer of ballots to Warehouse staff.

In OCROV's neighboring jurisdiction in Los Angeles County, helicopters would be used to transfer ballots from remote voting locations to its central office headquartered in Norwalk. At 4,060 square miles, Los Angeles County is significantly geographically larger than Orange County and has also more voters (approximately 6 million in 2020 compared to Orange County's 2 million).

No matter the distance or challenge, election officials understand the importance of returning voted ballots securely and efficiently.

INTERNAL SORTING

Once ballots were returned to the office, they would be moved immediately into a highly secure area of the Warehouse. Only those with approved badge access were able to enter the area, and this area was off-limits to observers. If anyone without badge access entered, they had to be accompanied by a staff member with badge access and approval to bring guests in.

Each Vote Center had its own "cage" where we would put voted ballots, conditional voter registrations and their corresponding ballots, and any other materials or equipment. This would be easy for staff to access and track which Vote Center's ballots, materials, and equipment were accounted for. Collection Center deliveries would be internally sorted and placed into these Vote Center cages. Hardware containing live ballots would be immediately brought to the Tally Room to be processed and added to the vote count.

ELECTION NIGHT GUESTS

On Election Night, election offices buzz with activity as various types of visitors come in to witness the results. Local observers, who may represent different organizations or groups, closely watch the proceedings to ensure transparency and fairness in the election process. Election attorneys are present to address any legal issues or disputes that may arise during the vote count.

Representatives from different political campaigns and partisan organizations also gathered at the elections office to monitor the results and gather possible insights for their respective parties. Additionally, media personnel were present to report on the election results as they unfolded, often making real-time calls on the outcome of specific races. For those unfamiliar with this process, media companies hire and send staff to key election offices around the country to report on election results. Instead of depending on websites or calling election officials for updates, media companies preferred having a person onsite at election offices to call in results and follow up with election officials should there be any confusion or issues.

International election observers were also present on election night to witness the democratic process in action. At this time, democracy in the United States was being closely watched by the global community to see if the civil unrest from the summer would impact election outcomes. They were there to observe the procedures, ensure transparency, and assess the integrity of the election. By being present at the central elections office, international election observers can gain firsthand experience of the American electoral system and its implementation. This on-the-ground experience allowed them to provide informed evaluations and recommendations based on their observations, which can be valuable for promoting best practices in elections worldwide and bring attention to any systemic issues.

Furthermore, it's not uncommon for federal agency representatives to be onsite to address security concerns and provide assistance if needed. Additionally, technical experts from voting equipment companies may be present to offer support and troubleshoot any technical issues that may arise during the election process. These diverse groups of visitors contribute to the dynamic atmosphere of the elections office on election night.

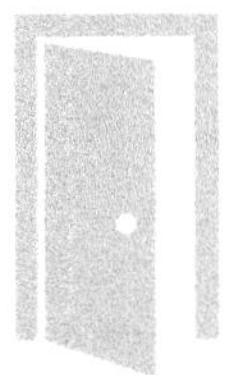

CLOSING THE DOORS ON ELECTION NIGHT

The central elections office continued to update election results on the hour until all voted ballots from Vote Centers were returned and processed. Since each Vote Center had its mini-storage unit onsite, most of the equipment and materials could be returned the next day. Previously, when Orange County operated one-day polling places, everything from a thousand polling places needed to be returned on Election Night and would often result in Election Night lasting until 2 a.m. or 3 a.m. the next day.

With the smaller number of voting locations and the addition of mini-storage units, Election Night was much more seamless and election officials and election workers had more time to take care of tasks and responsibilities. Although we had prepared for the worst, Election Day and Election Night were fortunately very smooth—there were just a few minor incidents and all resolved well in advance of the polls closing at 8 p.m.

Once all voted ballots were returned to the elections office, we began to close down Election Night operations and go through multiple checklists to ensure everything was covered. What media outlets, candidates, and campaigns cared most about after the unofficial election results were the remaining ballots to count. A separate team of election staff was identified for their strong attention to detail to count the remaining ballots, which would be posted on the website.

The remaining ballots to count were separated and counted by the following categories:

- ★ Total Ballots Left to Process

- ★ Vote-by-Mail Ballots Received on or Before Election Day via Mail Left to Process

- ★ Ballots from Drop Boxes Left to Process

- ★ Vote-by-Mail Returned at Vote Centers Left to Process

- ★ Duplicated Ballots Left to Process

- ★ Eligible Ballots Received After Election Day Left to Process

- ★ Conditional Voter Registrations and Provisional Ballots Left to Process

- ★ Final Drop Box Pickup Ballots Left to Process

- ★ Remote Accessible Vote-by-Mail Ballots Left to Process

The final election results would not be available until all remaining ballots were processed, verified, and counted. Knowing the amount of ballots left to count would indicate to the media, candidates, and campaigns whether there were enough unprocessed ballots to make a difference in specific contests. Typically, OCROV would update election results and the remaining ballots to count at 5 p.m. on weekdays and some weekends following Election Day.

After we released the final election results of the evening, we notified Election Night visitors over the intercom system that the office would be closing soon. I recall retreating to my office alone as most others were out in the Warehouse and by the Tally Room, where we had monitors displaying election results. I could hardly believe we reached this point.

Miraculously, I hadn't contracted COVID-19 in 2020 despite multiple scares and being around thousands of voters. For the most part, OCROV was very fortunate to maintain its operations and staffing despite some staff members having COVID-19 and being out for periods of time. Without vaccines available at the time, I knew it was a real possibility that contraction of COVID-19 could have resulted in death.

Despite the challenges of administering an election in a pandemic and during a time of civil unrest, we made it. We proved we could do it, and we did it well. We survived the protests, threats of violence, wildfires, and so much more. We ensured that every voter had access to the ballot box and made every effort to educate them and inform them of their voting options. We left no stone unturned in making voting easy, accessible, and secure. That should be the goal of every election official in every election.

As I sat alone in my office preparing myself to go back out for the final closing briefing, I felt at peace. I had given everything I could while serving in this election and it was enough. But I didn't do it alone. I felt immense appreciation for Neal, the management team I served with, OCROV staff and Extra Help, Vote Center CSRs and the Ballot Drop Box Strike Force Team, supportive media and external community partners, friends and family, and more who all made this possible. It was truly a community effort to ensure the 2020 Presidential General Election was safe, transparent, secure, and accessible to as many voters as possible.

I looked forward to closing the doors on Election Night, knowing that the elections office would be secured overnight with OCSD deputies guarding the premises. Our team would be ready to return in the morning to continue our processing and begin election canvass operations.

After the doors closed, I was excited to return home and see Howie soon. I looked forward to a hot shower, a hot meal, and a cozy and comfortable bed. The hardest part of this journey was over and we had given it all we could. And it was enough. We were and are enough.

We knew that we'd have to deal with more after Election Night, but there was no point in worrying about it right now. Whatever challenges we'd face, we'd overcome them together like we always do.

AFTERWORD

The 2020 Presidential General Election in Orange County, California had the highest voter turnout since the 1950s. Total turnout from the election was 87.3%, with 83% of voters casting the official ballot they had received through the mail and 17% casting their ballot in-person at one of 168 Vote Centers throughout Orange County.

Two months after the election, the January 6, 2021 Capitol Insurrection happened and it was a real wake-up call for our country. Though I was not in immediate danger, since I was 2,500 miles away from Washington, D.C. when this happened, it was immediately clear to me that this attack was an attack on democracy, elections, and its supporters. Unhappy with the election results, the insurrectionists were determined to prevent the certification of the electoral college votes by violently forcing their way into the Capitol with the intent of gravely harming our nation's leaders to get what they wanted.

After this event, I knew I wanted to play a more direct role in empowering communities and advocating for reforms that would expand and protect access to voting. Though I enjoyed working as an election official, I could not participate in political movements or express my personal beliefs and viewpoints to remain nonpartisan. I was ready for a change.

When I left my role at the Orange County Registrar of Voters in June 2021, I was a much different person than who I was when I started working there just four years prior. Being an election official and a senior manager challenged me in ways I did not expect and helped me grow to be the person I am today. I learned so much about elections and voting, even though I thought I had a solid grasp as someone who had previously worked in nonprofit advocacy, municipal government, and state government. I learned how to be an effective and strategic project manager, unafraid of political controversy, complexity, or tight deadlines. Enduring as much as I did as an election official also proved to me that I could overcome the toughest challenges and to believe in myself and my potential and to believe in our community and our community's potential.

Since leaving, I've started my own consultancy and have committed to work on projects that support election administrators, community advocates, and voters. I'm honored to have been trusted by values-led organizations to support their work in redistricting, community-responsive public governance, increasing voter registration at a university campus, a policy reform to implement Secure Automatic Voter Registration, and more. I'm excited for what the future holds and other opportunities to empower nonprofit organizations, communities, and leaders.

In addition, I have learned not to take my time with friends and family for granted. The anti-Asian sentiment at the time continued to grow during the time of the election and resulted in numerous acts of hate across the country. Though I did not personally experience a hate crime or flagrant discrimination, some of my friends and their families did and that was enough to affect my psyche. I worried about my parents, who were getting older and physically weaker. I worried that every time I saw them could be the last time. This experience has taught me to be grateful for my parents' good health, resilience, and support for me.

While I am not sure if I will return to work as an election official in the future, it will forever be an honor to have played a direct role in supporting transparent, secure, and accessible elections for the voters of Orange County. Whether as an election official, consultant, or another role, I remain committed to empowering our communities, ensuring their voices are heard, and changing systems to serve them. A brighter and more inclusive future will always be possible if we have hope and do the work to make it possible. I hope you'll join me in this commitment.

RESOURCES AND HOW TO GET INVOLVED

Nonpartisan voting resources are crucial for navigating voting and elections and understanding various roles and aspects of the U.S. government.

Here are some resources that offer explanations and general information for U.S. voters:

- ★ The Election Assistance Commission (https://www.eac. gov/) offers a wide variety of resources for voters:
  - o National Mail Voter Registration Form (https://eac. gov/voters/national-mail-voter-registration-form): The National Mail Voter Registration Form can be used to register U.S. citizens to vote, to update registration information due to a change of name, make a change of address or to register with a political party.
  - o Poll Worker Recruitment Lookup Tool (https://www. eac.gov/help-america-vote): The lookup tool helps individuals find information on being a poll worker in their community, including requirements, hours, pay, training, and more.

- o Voting Accessibility (https://www.eac.gov/voting-accessibility): This website provides information on how election officials ensure all voters can cast a ballot privately and independently.

- o Other National Contact Information (https://www.eac.gov/voters/other-national-contact-information): If you believe you have encountered misinformation or disinformation, voter intimidation, or voter fraud, please report these incidents to these national agencies and your local and state election offices.

- o Register And Vote in Your State (https://www.eac.gov/voters/register-and-vote-in-your-state): Each state and territory administers elections differently. Use this tool to find key dates and voting information about federal elections in all states and territories.

★ Your Democracy (https://whyy.org/programs/your-democracy/): PBS provides a five-part animated digital series on the branches of government, citizenship, voting rights, and more.

★ ALL IN Campus Democracy Challenge (https://allinchallenge.org/): Works with colleges and universities to achieve excellence in nonpartisan student democratic engagement

★ Better Civics (https://www.bettercivics.org/): Equips people with knowledge of how the government works at all levels.

★ Fact Check (https://www.factcheck.org/): Monitors factual accuracy of statements by major U.S. political major U.S. political figures.

* Guides.vote (https://guides.vote/): Produces nonpartisan voter guides that show where candidates stand.

* Institute for Responsive Government (https://responsivegov.org/): Helps policymakers find solutions that make government more efficient, accessible, and responsive to the needs of real human beings.

* The League of Women Voters (https://www.lwv.org/): Provides the general public with accessible voting education and resources to promote informed and active participation in the democratic process.

* Rock the Vote (https://rockthevote.org/): Uses pop culture, music, art, and technology to engage young people in politics and build their collective power.

* Students Learn Students Vote Coalition (https://slsvcoalition.org/): Helps campus and local leaders register and turn out more student voters every year.

* US Vote Foundation (https://www.usvotefoundation.org/): Provides online tools to assist U.S. citizens living anywhere in the world to register to vote and request their absentee ballot.

* Vote411 (https://www.vote411.org/): Provides nonpartisan information to the public with both general and state-specific information.

* Vote Smart (https://votesmart.org/): Provides free, factual, unbiased information on candidates and elected officials.

No Time to Fail (https://www.notimetofailfilm.com/) is a documentary that captures the commitment of Rhode Island's local election administrators and poll workers working around the clock to secure the vote for their community during the 2020 General Election. In this film, election administrators are highlighted as being on ground zero of democracy.

To learn more about how to become an election worker or poll worker, visit https://www.eac.gov/help-america-vote, or contact your local elections office and ask for more information.

Election official turnover has been increasing steadily since 2020. Turnover has roots in both long-standing and contemporary challenges. If you are seeking a rewarding career with opportunities to grow and truly make a difference in your community, please consider pursuing election administration as a career.

★ The Election Center and Auburn University partnered to offer a Professional Education Program (https://www.electioncenter.org/certified-elections-certifications.php), which is the first professional certification program for U.S. election and voter registration professionals. This graduate certificate is designed to provide students and practicing professionals with the knowledge, skills, and abilities to function effectively in election administration, specifically law and policy and critical contemporary issues facing the election administration community.

★ Electionline has a Jobs and Marketplace (https://electionline.org/jobs-marketplace/) listing of election official openings across the U.S.

★ The Humphrey School of Public Affairs at the University of Minnesota offers a Certificate in Election Administration. (https://www.hhh.umn.edu/certificate-programs/certificate-election-administration) This program was created in response to an urgent need for election professionals who are well trained in the latest technology and techniques in the field and well versed in the legal and policy challenges facing our voting system.

★ Georgia College & State University conducts a graduate Election Administration Certificate program. (https://www.gcsu.edu/artsandsciences/gov/graduate-election-administration-certificate) This program prepares students to facilitate democracy through critical analysis and public service in election administration.

ACKNOWLEDGMENTS

My grateful thanks to the incomparable Orange County Registrar of Voters team of 2020. Your dedication, kindness, and courage has enriched the pages of this book. My Outreach, Training, and Pop-Up Voting teams: thank you for trusting me to lead and provide guidance.

Neal Kelley, your leadership helped prepare me to overcome all of 2020's challenges and more. Your staunch commitment to providing the best possible voter experience for every voter is a high bar that every election official should strive to reach.

Thank you to Martha Bullen for your invaluable guidance in publishing this book and to Christy Day for your creative book cover and interior design. Much appreciation for David Aretha for your detailed editing in reviewing drafts of this book. Many thanks to Rebecca Lee and Eva Chen for their help in editing earlier drafts of this book.

Most importantly, I owe thanks to Howie, mentors, friends, and my family who provided support to me outside of the office in 2020.

Mike Adams, your unwavering support has helped me see more possibilities for myself than I knew possible. You have shown me the importance of relationships (as you are a super connector) and that personal development is just as important, if not more, as professional development. I am thankful for your mentorship and friendship over the past ten years.

It takes a special kind of person to mention your name in a room full of opportunity. Tammy Tran, I feel so fortunate to receive guidance and support from you when I was a legislative staffer, working at OCROV, and now as a consultant. You have paved the way for many young legislative staffers and women (like me), especially in Orange County.

I owe gratitude to countless friends and family members who checked in on me, checked in on Howie while I was working, dropped food off, and showed me grace when I was slow to respond to messages and missed social gatherings. I am truly blessed with wonderful beings who choose to be in community with me.

Dad, there are not enough words to thank you for the sacrifices you have made so that I could have a better life. Mom, you have modeled a carefree, independent, and joyful life and shown me it is possible for me too. I hope I have made you both proud and that I can live up to the hopes and dreams you had when you left Vietnam.

To my partner, Howie: you inspire me to reach my potential, and your love has changed me for the better in so many ways. I am grateful for your strong self of sense, willingness to go on adventures, and numerous talents and interests. For the countless times you've packed meals for me and my team, visited the office to brighten my day, held impromptu coaching sessions, reminded me to drink water and take a break, and so much more, you helped make sure that I was at my best and that I could overcome anything life threw at me in 2020 and more.

The Orange County Registrar of Voters' Vote Center Lab is a fully functional, permanent replica of an in-person voting location that supports testing of new processes and election worker training. Image credit: Orange County Registrar of Voters.

Orange County Registrar of Voters Neal Kelley, left, works with a film crew to film videos to inform voters and train election workers at the University Hills Community Center in Irvine, California. Image credit: Orange County Registrar of Voters.

Sample Vote Center layout used in the filming of election worker training videos. Image credit: Orange County Registrar of Voters.

Media representatives visit and film election worker training at the Orange County Registrar of Voters' warehouse in Santa Ana, California. Image credit: Orange County Registrar of Voters.

The Orange County Registrar of Voters' "I Voted" sticker inflatable is placed at the front of the Honda Center in Anaheim, California. Image credit: Orange County Registrar of Voters.

ORANGE COUNTY'S
VOTE CENTER SUPER SITE
FRIDAY, OCTOBER 30TH - TUESDAY, NOVEMBER 3RD

The Orange County Registrar of Voters partnered with the Anaheim Ducks to promote the Honda Center as "Orange County's Vote Center Super Site" during the 2020 Presidential General Election. Image credit: Orange County Registrar of Voters.

116 official ballot drop boxes were available for voters to use to return ballots in the 2020 Presidential General Election in Orange County, California. Image credit: Orange County Registrar of Voters.

Pop-up mobile voting setup at the Laguna Niguel Regional Park in Laguna Niguel, California. Image credit: Orange County Registrar of Voters.

A press conference is being held on Orange County's comprehensive plans to safeguard the election by Secretary of State Alex Padilla, Orange County Registrar of Voters Neal Kelley, and Orange County District Attorney Todd Spitzer at the Orange County Registrar of Voters' office in Santa Ana, California. Image credit: Orange County Registrar of Voters.

Nearly two million county voter information guides are stored in the Orange County Registrar of Voters' warehouse in Santa Ana, California, before being mailed out to voters. Image credit: Orange County Registrar of Voters.

These Vote Center Customer Service Representatives from the Irvine City Hall Vote Center team are a part of the 1,500 election workers hired and trained to assist voters in the 2020 Presidential General Election. Image credit: Orange County Registrar of Voters.

Healthcare professionals take a photo after voting in front of the pop-up mobile voting unit at the St. Jude Medical Center in Fullerton, California. Image credit: Orange County Registrar of Voters.

Due to the Silverado Fire,
we are cancelling
today's voting event.

For more information,
call **714-567-7600**

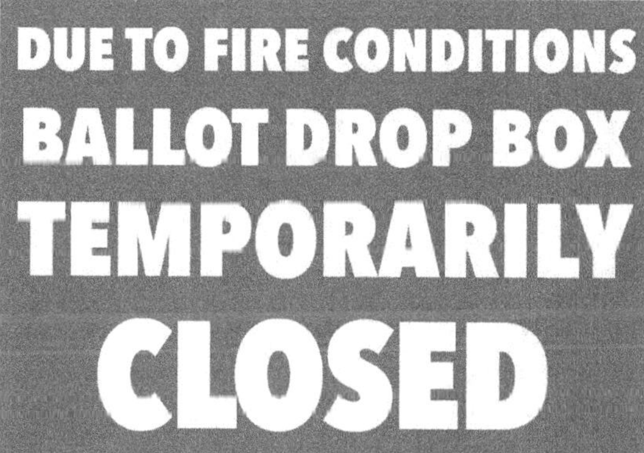

The Orange County Registrar of Voters developed signage to notify the public of a closed ballot drop box and canceled pop-up voting event. Image credit: Orange County Registrar of Voters.

Pop-up mobile voting setup at Main Place Mall in Santa Ana, California. Image credit: Orange County Registrar of Voters.

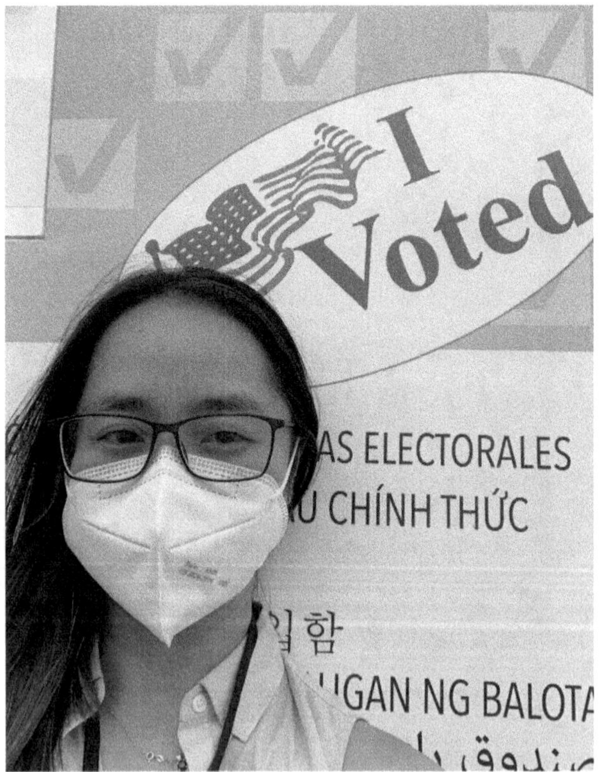

Jackie Wu sits in front of a ballot drop box during a filming break.

ABOUT THE AUTHOR

JACKIE WU is an experienced consultant specializing in nonprofit advocacy, voter outreach and engagement, and election administration. She previously worked as the Community Outreach manager for the Orange County Registrar of Voters, the fifth-largest voting jurisdiction in the United States, from 2017 to 2021. During this time, Jackie was responsible for overseeing the translation of election materials into nine languages, election worker training, pop-up voting, social media, media, legislation, and outreach to approximately two million voters.

Following the highly controversial and scrutinized 2020 General Election, Jackie was deeply impacted by the false accusations of voting and election fraud that sought to undermine voting rights. She experienced an epiphany after the January 6, 2021 Capitol insurrection. Jackie felt called to apply her experiences and knowledge to play a more direct role in empowering historically excluded communities to realize their political power and potential.

A daughter of Chinese Vietnamese refugees, Jackie is a graduate of UC Irvine with a bachelor's degree in Political Science. She earned a certificate in Advanced Public Engagement for Local Government from Pepperdine University and a certificate in Applied Compassion from Stanford University. Jackie's past work experiences include working as a government administrator at the municipal level and for the California State Senate. She has been featured on NPR as well as in the *Los Angeles Times* and CalMatters, and she has offered presentations and workshops on voting and the election process to numerous organizations.

Jackie lives in Orange County, California and spends her free time traveling, swimming, and playing pickleball. For more information or to contact Jackie, visit www.jwuconsulting.com.